D1575688

History of Carver School of Missions
and Social Work

History of
Carver School of Missions
and Social Work

———————— ◇ ————————

CARRIE U. LITTLEJOHN

BROADMAN PRESS
Nashville, Tennessee

Library of Congress Card Catalog Number: 58–8923

Printed in the United States of America

3.5JN58K.S.P.

Contents

v

This Book Is Affectionately Dedicated to
THE STUDENTS
of
Woman's Missionary Union Training School
and
Carver School of Missions and Social Work
Who for Fifty Years Have Embodied Its Ideals

Foreword

IT HAS BEEN A REVEALING EXPERIENCE to trace the history of Carver School of Missions and Social Work from its small beginning at the turn of the century to its fiftieth anniversary year.

At the risk of being tedious, I have tried to give the facts as I have found them in original sources: the minutes of the WMU Executive Committee and of the annual meetings of Woman's Missionary Union, the minutes and reports of the Board of Trustees and the local Board of Managers. Much use has also been made of articles appearing in denominational papers from 1900 to 1907.

The story of the growth and development of any school is to be found, for the most part, in the biographies of the men and women who have set its policies and guided its destiny. This story, therefore, deals largely with the human element: the founders, the men who have served as counselors, the Board of Trustees, the faculty, the staff, the students, and the loyal constituency. Personal acquaintance with many of the men and women connected with the school may have given a personal bias, though I have tried to be fair. The lack of space has ruled out the full story of the contributions of many individuals who have served the school with dedicated devotion.

I am greatly indebted to many persons and groups for help in collecting the material and preparing the manuscript: the staff at WMU headquarters; friends at Carver School; the staffs of the libraries of the Southern Baptist Theological Seminary, the Baptist Sunday School Board, and Furman University; the WMU office in South Carolina; Miss Willie Jean Stewart; and others too numerous to mention.

CARRIE U. LITTLEJOHN

Introduction

WOMAN'S MISSIONARY UNION takes delight in presenting to
the readers of this history the School whose story it records
and the author who recorded it.

At a time when doors to seminaries were not open to women,
Woman's Missionary Union recognized that God's call to definite Christian service was not restricted to men. Its leaders
foresaw the approaching day when opportunities for certain
types of service could best be met by women if women could
be properly trained. The history unfolds the chapters in the
evolution of Southern Baptists' first training school, known
originally as Woman's Missionary Union Training School for
Christian Workers. Within the covers of the book are bound
fifty years of progress in the preparation of over four thousand
women for the roles they were to play in the life of our denomination and the forward march of missions. More than four
hundred of these women have received appointment to missionary service. This eventful half-century has witnessed the
operation of the school by Louisville Baptist women and
Woman's Missionary Union, and has brought it to the day
when the Southern Baptist Convention assumed the responsibility for its operation.

Reflected in this book is a constancy of purpose in the
minds and hearts of the school's founders, leaders, and students
through the years of beginnings, growth, crises, pioneering, and
transition. This intimate account is alive with portraits of
missionary statesmen and individuals whose names have been

synonymous with missionary education and who have envisioned a ministry to all areas of life. Projected vividly are the life and traditions of the school from its beginning.

It is one thing to tell the story of a school and another thing to live it. Dr. Carrie U. Littlejohn has done both. She is not only an educator, but her own scholastic pursuits have been constant. She attended Converse College, received a bachelor of religious education degree from Hartford School of Religious Education, and a master's degree from Northwestern University. In 1944 Georgetown College conferred upon her the honorary degree of Doctor of Laws. At the time of her retirement from the presidency of the school in 1951 she returned to her home in Spartanburg, South Carolina.

Arriving at "House Beautiful" in 1913, Carrie Littlejohn was described by Mrs. E. Y. Mullins as having a face "intelligent and arresting . . . her manner both reserved and frank—merry and shy." She was a conscientious student and in 1915 became a graduate of the Training School. Evidencing exceptional maturity and capability, she was made director of the Training School Good Will Center in 1921, associate principal of the school in 1925, and administrative head in 1930. The events of this history and the life of the author stand inseparable. Sensing the needs of her generation, Miss Littlejohn stood with uncalculated love and courage as an example of unselfish devotion through dark hours as well as in glowing successes. Tributes have been numerous, but perhaps the words of Dr. W. O. Carver adequately capture the spirit of this author: "She was a personality . . . but never a dominating personality . . . never a self-conscious personality . . . and never used her personality to impose her will . . . The other impression which is at the center of her personality is genuineness."

ALMA HUNT
Executive Secretary
Woman's Missionary Union

1

A Venture of Faith

Nothing in life is more wonderful than faith—the
one great moving force which we can neither
weigh in the balance nor test in the crucible.—
SIR WILLIAM OSLER

A SIGNIFICANT ANNIVERSARY YEAR, the fiftieth of the Carver
School of Missions and Social Work, closed in May, 1957, with
a fitting celebration in Chicago during the annual session of
Woman's Missionary Union. In May, 1907, this beloved institution began its work as the Woman's Missionary Union Training School under sponsorship of Woman's Missionary Union.

In her account of the adoption of the little school in 1907,
Fannie E. S. Heck labeled the action a "venture of faith." She
had originally used that expression at the meeting in Richmond when she said, "Without a building, without a faculty,
with no money, we have agreed to build and operate a school.
It is a venture of faith."

For fifty years the institution was generously supported, lovingly guided, and fondly cherished by the parent organization because of the opportunities for missionary service that
it provided. The time came, however, when changing conditions and developments within the denominational program
indicated that a school dedicated to the missionary training of
women only had fulfilled its original mission. On the other
hand, unprecedented missionary opportunities pointed out an
unmet need in an expanding missionary program. It seemed
that the time was ripe for a new venture of faith—a school ded-

1

icated to the specific and advanced training of the hundreds of men and women needed in missionary service at home and around the world.

But that story must wait for a review of the facts concerning the birth and growth of the training school movement in Southern Baptist life.

Roots in the Past

To understand why Carver School of Missions and Social Work came into being it is necessary to turn the pages of history back to the nineteenth century. While 1907 marked its beginning as an organized, independent school, the school's roots go far back into the past. A developing missionary awakening made it a necessity.

In his *History of the Expansion of Christianity* Dr. K. S. Latourette labels the nineteenth century the "great century, the greatest thus far in the history of Christianity." Basic in the forces that made it so was the religious awakening that profoundly affected the Christian life of the Western world, particularly of the United States. Dr. Latourette points out further that Christianity "had never been so much alive. . . . had never been so vigorous, not even in its idealized first centuries." [1] After the spiritual stagnation of the eighteenth century this revival was dramatic and far-reaching.

Leading in this nineteenth-century religious awakening were the great preachers, notably Finney, Spurgeon, and Moody. This revival spirit did not die with them. Its continuing influence was reflected in an article, "Whole World in a Revival," by Dr. W. O. Carver, a young professor at the Southern Baptist Theological Seminary. He said in part, "There is a great Christian revival on in the Christian lands, but it is also obvious to the student of religions that there is a religious revival throughout the world. . . . What shall be the outcome of the awakening in our time?" [2]

The genuineness of the religious revival in the Western

world was demonstrated by a deepened interest in foreign missions. During the nineteenth century, through migration of Christian groups and direct missionary effort, "Christian communities arose in almost every island, land, tribe and nation." [3]

When there is a religious revival, it is inevitable that there will follow a new interest in missions. Dr. A. J. Brown pointed out fifty years ago that:

It was not an accident . . . or a mere coincidence that the forward movement in missions that characterized the closing years of that century [the nineteenth] dated from the extraordinary revivals of 1875–76. The teaching of history on this subject is unbroken. Every deepening of the spiritual life has been followed by a new effort to give the gospel to the world. [4]

The story of the foreign mission movement in the nineteenth century is largely the story of missionaries whose heroic service stirred the imagination and emotions of the Christian world. The names of Robert Moffat, David Livingstone, Robert Morrison, and John G. Paton focused the attention of Christian college students on the whole world.

Ann and Adoniram Judson and Luther Rice aroused American Baptists to face their responsibility in the great missionary enterprise. One result of their efforts was the organization of the American Baptist Foreign Mission Society. Henrietta Hall and J. Lewis Shuck, of Virginia, brought foreign missions into the spiritual vision of Baptists in the South by going to China under the American Baptist Foreign Mission Society. China became a challenging mission field, especially for women, as this heroic young woman, still in her teens, became America's first woman missionary to that vast country in the Orient.

During the last quarter of this great century another Virginian, Lottie Moon, went to China. Her influence has probably been more fruitful among Southern Baptists than that of any other missionary.

One of the most far-reaching developments of the missionary awakening of the nineteenth century was the organization of the Student Volunteer Movement in 1886 at Mt. Hermon, Massachusetts. This fellowship united and channeled the dedicated zeal of college students into world missions.

The first meeting of the group was attended by 250 young men and women from colleges of Canada and the United States. The missionary spirit implanted in this relatively small group was carried back to the colleges to inspire and enlist an ever-enlarging army of students in a great missionary crusade.

The values of this first meeting were conserved by a practical follow-up program to lead Christian students to a consideration of foreign missions as a life work, to foster the purpose of those who should decide to become missionaries, to guide and stimulate them through mission study, to unite all volunteers in an organized, aggressive movement, and to create an intelligent, active interest in foreign missions among students who remained in the home field.

Following this first significant student meeting, quadrennial conferences continued to be held regularly in order to reach each college generation. The impact of these conferences on students at the turn of the century was tremendous. At the meeting in Toronto in 1902, definite prayer was made for one thousand students to go out as foreign missionaries in the four years ahead.

At the meeting held in Nashville in 1906, it was reported that the one thousand had gone out, one-third of them women. Among this number were young women from Southern Baptist churches who had gone for special training to Northern Baptist schools, or had "picked up" what they could at the Southern Baptist Theological Seminary, or had stumbled into the work of a foreign missionary without benefit of any special training.

The emergence of women in missions in the nineteenth century was a vital part of the total picture of the changing position of woman in the Western world. The crusade on the part of women during that revolutionary era "impressed itself on

4

the public mind in a series of claims to equal citizenship—in politics, education, professional and industrial employment, legal status, social respect. But these practical claims add up at a deeper level to one demand: the recognition of woman's full share in a common humanity." [5]

To the devoted Christian woman this urge for a full share in a common humanity found its satisfaction in sharing with women in pagan and heathen lands the experience that had lifted her out of a position of inferiority to one of equality in life and service.

While her American and British sisters were supporting the suffrage movement and various humanitarian projects in an effort to secure equal citizenship, the missionary-minded Christian woman found her "freedom of action . . . achieved through demonstration of efficiency in service. . . . The demonstration of woman's opportunities and responsibilities in Christian service found their first realizations in missions." [6]

The quiet but courageous work of Mary Webb, of Massachusetts, who from a wheel chair organized more than a hundred missionary societies among women and children, preceded by a half-century the militant campaign for woman's suffrage of Susan B. Anthony of the same state. The movement that began to engage the dedicated devotion of women to missions was fifty years old when Florence Nightingale electrified the world by taking over the responsibility of nursing the soldiers in the Crimean War in 1854.

Mary Webb's example brought results far beyond her limited circle of personal influence. Missionary societies were organized in eleven states of the South by 1840. The first meeting of Southern Baptist women in the interest of missions was held in Baltimore in 1868 during the session of the Southern Baptist Convention. The women attending the Convention were asked to meet in the basement of a church to pray especially for missions in China. At the meeting they were urged to ask their societies to contribute to the support of Bible women in China.

At the request of the Foreign Mission Board in 1874 central committees were appointed to foster women's work in the United States. This fostering was fruitful, for by 1888, when Woman's Missionary Union was organized, more than twelve hundred societies for women and children were reported.

As Carver School of Missions and Social Work is viewed against this "great century" background, there is a sense of its permanence and stability. It was no sudden sprouting of seed in rocky ground, but rather the sturdy growth of a plant rooted in the good soil of human need and aspiration.

The general revival prepared hearts and minds for a great missionary awakening. The organization of women and children focused attention on the need for missionaries and for money to support them. The Student Volunteer Movement enlisted young men and women in the cause of missions. The need for women in the expanding foreign missionary enterprise was making its appeal to young women to prepare for this heroic service.

The time was ripe for the starting of a special school of missionary training among Southern Baptists. Mission work pointed out the need, and courageous and dedicated young women brought the issue into the open as they went to Louisville to attend seminary classes.

The movement to free woman from the age-old shackles, beginning back in the nineteenth century, had to jump many hurdles. In the fields of suffrage and social status, it was a militant movement. In church circles, a different approach was made. Woman quietly did what she could without the benefit of masculine approval until Christian courtesy demanded that she be accepted "on a basis of equality in worth, in grace, in privilege, where each according to fitness and spiritual gifts was to find and fill the appropriate and effective function for the growth of the Body of Christ." [7]

Conservative minds change slowly, but they change when the arguments are convincing. The time came when Southern

Baptist men began to recognize woman's place in the work of the church, and especially in Christian missions. This awareness brought them to take their stand among the friends of the movement to provide missionary training for the woman volunteer. An excerpt from an article in the *Biblical Recorder* reveals the trend of the thinking of men of the period on this vital subject.

Speaking of the Training School for Young Women in our Seminary, the *Biblical Recorder* says: "This is only a reasonable—indeed a necessary—recognition of woman's larger place in our Christian economy. On the mission field she has long been indispensable. And it is indispensable that we train her for her work on the mission field. Likewise she has proved herself, beyond all doubt, of great value in Sunday-school teaching, church (personal) missionary work, and in the school-room. And if she has her place in these important fields, it is worthwhile—it is necessary—to train her, to give her the best training in the world." [8]

It took years of struggle on the part of Southern Baptist young women and six years of active effort by a small group of leading men in the denomination to bring men and women in places of responsibility to support openly the idea of a training school for women.

The Training School Movement

At the turn of the century, when leaders in Southern Baptist circles began to take seriously the idea of starting a training school for women, the movement was already well established in the program of Northern Baptists and other evangelical denominations. The Baptist Missionary Training School in Chicago was founded in 1881 under the auspices of the Woman's American Baptist Home Mission Society.

In 1890 the Woman's American Baptist Foreign Mission Society established a home at Newton Center, Massachusetts, where women under appointment for foreign service might spend a year while attending classes in Newton Theological

Seminary. The experiment was so successful that in 1895 the Society built Hasseltine House so that all of their young women planning to do mission work might have the privilege of one or two years of study in the Newton Seminary.

The Baptist Training School for Christian Workers in Philadelphia, later called the Baptist Institute, was founded in 1892.

The women of the Southern Methodist Church established Scarritt Bible and Training School in Kansas City in 1892. It was moved to Nashville in 1924 and renamed Scarritt College for Christian Workers. At that time its course of study was reorganized and the school enlarged as a senior college and graduate school for training both men and women for missionary service.

The Brooklyn Union Missionary Training Institute (interdenominational) appears to have been well established by 1904. Other schools in existence at this time were the Episcopal Training School for women missionaries in New York and a training school for Methodist deaconesses in Washington, D. C. The Presbyterians did not start their schools until the early part of the twentieth century.

Women at the Seminary

The attendance of women in the classes of the Southern Baptist Theological Seminary began well back in the nineteenth century. Mrs. E. Y. Mullins, in her history of the first twenty-five years of the Training School, tells of a young woman who attended Seminary classes as early as the session of 1884–1885.

In a leaflet issued by the Seminary faculty during the controversy over the beginning of a training school for women, Dr. Mullins said, "Women have been attending the lecture courses in the Seminary for many years. In the days of Drs. Boyce and Broadus and the earlier Faculty women were frequently admitted to the lecture courses in the Seminary." [9]

Dr. W. O. Carver, in his Founders' Day address on October 2, 1948, said, "From, at least, as early as 1891 married women had been attending Seminary classes with their husbands, and occasionally, also, some unmarried women had listened quietly to lectures."

The quiet listening, which was innate and natural in those young women of the Victorian age, came to be a policy for women students which carried over into later years. It was impressed upon Training School students that they were guests in the Seminary classes, and so they must not take up the time of the professors or make themselves conspicuous by asking questions. The shy student did not object to this prohibition. Indeed, she was panic-stricken when called on to recite in the large classes where women were always in the minority. The more aggressive young woman, however, or the one whose thirst for knowledge overshadowed her acquired feeling of inferiority experienced frustration under the limitations put upon her. The time came when she would no longer accept the assumption that she was a second-rate member of the classes.

One Man's Idea

It has been accepted as a fact from the very beginning of the Training School that Dr. E. Z. Simmons, pioneer missionary to China, was the father of the idea of a missionary training school for women among Southern Baptists. Early records, however, bring to light an interesting resolution which reveals that the Woman's Missionary Union of Texas was about five years earlier than Dr. Simmons in proposing such a school. At the meeting of the Executive Committee of Woman's Missionary Union in Baltimore in November, 1895, the following resolution was presented:

Resolved, that the Baptist Woman's Missionary Union of Texas encourage the establishment of a Baptist Missionary Training School for young women; that the school be centrally located between the east and west lines of Southern Baptist Convention territory; that a copy of this resolution be forwarded to the Corresponding Secretary of Woman's Missionary Union, Auxiliary to the Southern Baptist Convention.

On motion of Miss Annie Armstrong it was decided to reply that the committee had considered the resolution in regard to a training school, but for the present deemed it not wise to undertake new work, and would recommend the Chicago and Philadelphia training schools open to workers.[10]

Dr. Simmons, of Mississippi, was appointed as a missionary to China in 1870. Through thirty years of pioneer work he had earned the respect and confidence not only of his fellow missionaries but also of leaders in the home field. During these years he had observed the difficulties under which women missionaries worked because of their poor preparation. For a long time he had considered the problem and sought a solution. Finally, he decided that the time was ripe for constructive action. While on furlough from May, 1899, to October, 1900, he carried on an aggressive campaign for the establishment of a training school in connection with the Seminary in Louisville.

Dr. Simmons visited Louisville early in 1900 for the purpose of conferring with the Seminary faculty regarding the matter. Dr. Mullins was out of the city at the time, but Dr. Simmons found other members of the faculty heartily in favor of the idea. Realizing the importance of taking a group of women into his confidence at the very beginning, he presented the project to the missionary societies of Broadway and Walnut Street Baptist churches and found these women ready to cooperate. He made concrete suggestions as to the rental of a house near the Seminary large enough to care for twelve or fifteen women. He outlined a suggested course of study and explained that there would be a need not only for a matron but also for a "good practical woman" who would live in the home and teach the practical courses not offered at the Seminary.

Immediately after this visit to Louisville Dr. Simmons wrote

10

to Dr. Willingham, secretary of the Foreign Mission Board, and Miss Annie Armstrong, secretary of Woman's Missionary Union. He knew that he must secure the interest and co-operation of these two key people before going further. He told them of his recent visit to Louisville and of the enthusiastic response of the Seminary faculty and the women of Broadway and Walnut Street churches.

Dr. Willingham and Miss Armstrong promptly wrote to Dr. Mullins to ascertain his reaction to Dr. Simmons' idea. Dr. Mullins replied to these letters in a cordial manner with assurances of the Seminary's interest and co-operation. He made it clear, however, that the Seminary could not assume any responsibility, financial or otherwise, for a woman's department. In a frank way he put the responsibility where he and his faculty thought it belonged. In the letter to Miss Armstrong he said in part,

It seems to me the most logical arrangement would be for the Woman's Missionary Union to take the matter in hand, and through a strong committee it could easily do what might need to be done. But unless someone shall be charged with the financial responsibility connected with the movement, and its general oversight, it is not likely to be satisfactory in all respects.[11]

One Woman's Conviction

From the beginning of the movement in 1900 by Dr. Simmons the faculty and trustees of the Seminary, the secretaries of the boards, and other leaders in the denomination, both men and women, felt that the project should be underwritten by Woman's Missionary Union. It was woman's work for women, they all agreed. In fact, approval of Dr. Simmons' idea appeared to be unanimous except for one important person, Miss Armstrong. At first she seemed to have an open mind on the matter, but by the time the WMU Executive Committee in Baltimore met in its April session in 1900, her opposition had apparently crystallized.

11

At the March meeting of the committee, following the exciting exchange of letters among Dr. Simmons, Dr. Willingham, Dr. Mullins, and Miss Armstrong, letters concerning the training school were read from Dr. Simmons and from Dr. Willingham; Mrs. Cushing of Oklahoma, Miss Eliza Broadus of Kentucky, and Miss Burdette of the Baptist Missionary Training School in Chicago.

The record of the April meeting states that "Miss Armstrong reported a busy month, it being near the close of the year, and also much work had to be done in connection with the plan for Training School." She reported further that Dr. Simmons had met the secretaries of the Home and Foreign Mission boards in Georgia, and in this conference it was decided to present the plan for a training school in Louisville to the two boards at their spring meetings.

In the extended discussion on the school issue, letters were read from a Mr. Hamilton of Louisville, Dr. Willingham, Dr. Kerfoot, Mrs. Cushing, Miss Burdette, Mrs. Stakely, and others. In conclusion the record states, "On motion of Mrs. Tyler it was decided that the Executive Committee after careful consideration at two meetings are opposed to starting a training school for women at any place at the present." The group made clear their position in a final motion, made by Mrs. Nimmo, "that if there is to be a training school, Louisville is not the place." [12]

And that settled the matter, as far as the WMU Executive Committee was concerned, for several years. It also put a damper on the whole movement. At the WMU Executive Committee on June 12, it was reported that the Foreign Mission Board had deferred the matter of the training school, and it was not discussed at the spring meeting of the Home Board. In view of Miss Armstrong's opposition, no one, apparently, had the courage to bring the question to the annual session of Woman's Missionary Union.

What were Miss Armstrong's reasons for being so violently opposed to locating the training school in Louisville? We are dependent upon the reports of her contemporaries, for we have no word from her fully clarifying her position.

An article by Dr. T. P. Bell, at that time editor of the *Christian Index,* describing a visit he made to the Seminary and the training school home in 1906, notes the major objections to locating the school in Louisville. These may well be a repetition of Miss Armstrong's expressed objections. He said:

. . . We had heard of its being charged against this Training School that it would prove a sort of match-making institution . . . The great fear that this would be the case has always seemed to us an absurd one. It might well have arisen in the fertile imagination of some maiden lady of uncertain age . . . What if a few of the students [of the Seminary] and of these young women should marry? Is that reason for opposing so good an institution? . . . For our part, while we have no fear at all of the Training School becoming a match-making bureau, we should be far from grieving if some of the young ministers at the Seminary should marry some of these consecrated and well-trained young women, in preference to some of the giddy girls who some times catch the fancy even of the young "theolog."

We had also heard the charge made against this school that the young women were being trained to be preachers. Absurd also is this suggestion, evidently diligently sought by some one who was striving to prejudice people against a good institution, against which no real objections could be found. . . .

Still another objection that has been urged against this school is that it is the project of a number of ladies in Louisville, Ky. What if it is, if so be that it is a good institution, doing good work? But the facts are against any such charge.[13]

Dr. W. O. Carver, for many years associated with the school, said that Miss Armstrong's main objection was that the school would become a matrimonial bureau if it were located in Louisville.

A Venture in Faith

The whirlwind campaign to establish a training school for women continued from January through April in 1900. Dis-

13

couraged over his failure to receive the co-operation of Miss Armstrong, Dr. Simmons apparently gave up the struggle. The faculty of the Seminary and the secretaries of the boards likewise let the matter drop. At this stage, however, another influential group of men, the Board of Trustees of the Seminary, took action. At their annual meeting in New Orleans in May, 1901,

A resolution was introduced looking toward the establishment of the woman's training school in connection with the Seminary. A committee of three members of the Board of Trustees [Dr. W. E. Hatcher, Judge A. D. Freeman, and Dr. A. J. Holt], was appointed to consider the matter one year and report. At the next annual meeting of the Board held in Asheville, North Carolina, in 1902, the report was submitted, recommending the opening of the doors of the Seminary to women desiring training, and was unanimously adopted by the Board. . . . When action was taken establishing the school, announcements were made to that effect, and at the opening of the next session women were admitted according to the instructions of the Board.[14]

In the 1902–1903 session women were for the first time enrolled in the classes and given the privilege of taking examinations, but they were not matriculated as students. Their names were printed in the next catalog in a separate list.

This historic action of the Board of Trustees to admit women as members of the classes, though not as students in the Seminary, proved to be a definite forward step in the beginning of the training school. It probably served, however, to delay the entering of Woman's Missionary Union into the project. This development was used by the opposition during the controversy from 1903 to 1907 to prove that since a training school was already being operated by the Seminary, Woman's Missionary Union did not need to do anything about it.

A Venture in Courage

If a small group of men dared to act on faith rather than see the movement die by default, a group of women added courage to their faith by bringing the question into the annual meeting of WMU in Savannah in 1903. In spite of the fact that the WMU Executive Committee had taken a positive stand against the proposed training school in 1900, there were women throughout the South who felt that such a school was needed and that Woman's Missionary Union should do something about it. Accordingly, an item in the program that year served to turn the spotlight on the issue. One report of the meeting said that "a most interesting paper, 'The Demand for Trained Women Workers, How to Meet It,' was read by Mrs. George W. Truett of Texas." Out of the discussion the following resolution, later passed by the Convention, was adopted by the Union,

That the Southern Baptist Convention be requested to appoint a committee of seven—three of whom shall be the Secretaries of the Foreign, Home and Sunday School Boards—to confer with a committee of the same size, appointed by the Woman's Missionary Union, to consider the advisability of establishing a Missionary Training School for women; said committee to report at the meeting of the Convention in 1904, and at the annual meeting of the Woman's Missionary Union the same year, and, if favorable, to suggest place of location, nature of operating, method of raising funds, etc., etc.[15]

Mrs. John H. Eager, vice-president from Maryland, was presiding in the absence of the president. As a sister-in-law of Mrs. George B. Eager she was thoroughly conversant with the situation in Louisville and altogether in favor of Woman's Missionary Union's taking over the responsibility. She, therefore, appointed a strong and representative committee. Courtesy or custom led her to name Miss Armstrong as a member of the committee and to call her name first. Miss Armstrong became the chairman of the committee and its spokesman at the 1904 annual session in Nashville.

The committee appointed by the president of the Southern Baptist Convention to confer with the WMU committee on this important matter included W. J. Northen, J. B. Hawthorne, A. J. S. Thomas, J. N. Prestridge, and the secretaries of the three boards, R. J. Willingham, F. C. McConnell, and J. M. Frost.

Dr. Prestridge, editor of the *Baptist Argus,* published in Louisville, emerged as the spokesman of this Southern Baptist Convention committee of seven. Shortly before the Nashville meetings of the Southern Baptist Convention and Woman's Missionary Union, when the joint committee would make its report, he promoted an aggressive program to win support for the project. He asked Dr. Mullins to write for the April 7 issue of his paper an article on the subject, "Training School for Women." In the article Dr. Mullins said, "There are very many strong considerations in favor of Louisville as the location for the training school for women. Not the least of these is that we already have such a successful training school in connection with our work in the Seminary." [16] Unfortunately, this statement was used in the committee meeting in Nashville a few weeks later by Miss Armstrong to nullify the very purpose of the committee. If there was already a successful training school being carried on by the Seminary, why should a committee discuss the advisability of establishing a missionary training school? And what mere man or group of men could answer that argument!

In a final effort to interest the denomination in the idea before the meeting of the joint committee in Nashville, Dr. Prestridge devoted the entire issue of the *Argus* for May 5, 1904, to the proposed training school. As an introduction he said in his "Notes and Comments" column:

We have no idea that the Seminary wishes to force itself on the women in the matter of the Woman's Training School, but is simply at the service of the women if they wish to come here. As we understand it, if the school is located in Louisville, it will have its own board of managers, its own home, its matron and teachers, its own financial responsibility, and give its own certificates. Only in the matter of teaching, the classes of the Seminary are open free of charge wherever the teaching fits in with the aims of the Training School.[17]

The leading article in the *Argus*, "The Missionary Training School," was apparently written by Dr. Prestridge. Dr. R. J. Willingham of the Foreign Mission Board expressed his convictions in an article, "Our Training School for Women Should Be as Good as the Men's." There were articles on the Baptist Missionary Training School in Chicago by Dr. Johnston Myers, a Baptist pastor in Chicago, and Miss Annie Jenkins of Texas (later Mrs. W. E. Sallee of China) who was at that time a student in the Chicago school.

The work of the Baptist Training School in Philadelphia was presented by Miss Frances Schuyler, its preceptress. Dr. W. G. Partridge, a pastor in Pittsburgh, who had known both the Chicago and the Philadelphia schools at close range, put his stamp of approval on these schools in his article, "How They Work." Hasseltine House at Newton Center, supported by the Woman's Baptist Foreign Mission Society, was described as a missionary experiment by Miss Lydia Edmonds. One interdenominational school, the Brooklyn Union Missionary Training Institute, was presented by its vice-principal, Miss Hester Alway.

Finally, Dr. Prestridge sought to clinch the whole argument by securing the endorsement of many leaders among Southern Baptist women: Mrs. W. E. Hatcher of Virginia, Mrs. J. F. Love of Arkansas, Mrs. A. J. Wheeler of Tennessee, Miss Eliza Broadus of Kentucky, Mrs. C. V. Edwards of Louisiana, and Miss Julia McKenzie, missionary to China.

Why did Dr. Prestridge's well-planned strategy fail? Was the joint committee intimidated by Miss Armstrong's determined opposition and dominating personality? The only report on the committee meeting is found in Dr. Prestridge's report on the Convention at Nashville in which he rather meekly states:

The Woman's Missionary Training School was committed to the Seminary by both the Convention and the Woman's Missionary Union. . . . The Woman's Missionary Training School matter was quickly settled. Miss Annie Armstrong, of the W.M.U., offered in the committee a resolution committing for the present the entire matter to the Seminary. There were some differences of opinion, but we will all endorse the action of the Seminary trustees in founding a training school, which action was unanimously heartily endorsed by the Convention. We bespeak the prayers and help of our sisters over the states. We will not look to them in vain.[18]

The WMU minutes include the following record:

Report of Committee on Training School was presented by Miss A. W. Armstrong, Md., and the following Resolution adopted:

Whereas, no notice had been given that there was a Training School for women missionaries in connection with the Southern Baptist Theological Seminary at Louisville, Ky., prior to the appointment of the joint committee by Southern Baptist Convention and Woman's Missionary Union, May, 1903, to consider the advisability of establishing a Missionary Training School for Women, said Committee to report at meeting of the Convention 1904, and the annual meeting of Woman's Missionary Union the same year:

And Whereas, Dr. E. Y. Mullins, President of the Theological Seminary, makes public in "Baptist Argus," April 7, 1904: "We already have such a successful Training School in connection with our work at the Seminary";

Be it resolved: That no action be taken by the Committee, but that the whole subject be left with the Seminary for the present.[19]

At the Convention in Nashville, "President Northen reported that no action had been taken on the request of the Woman's Missionary Union for the establishment of a training school for women in Louisville, as one was already in existence." [20]

Dr. J. M. Frost, secretary of the Sunday School Board, and

like Dr. Prestridge deeply concerned about the whole matter, was not willing that a movement that had such promise at the preceding Convention should be resolved into oblivion in this fashion. He therefore offered a new resolution that not only kept the movement alive but also opened the way for any and all Southern Baptists who might be interested to contribute to the support of the homeless infant school that had been left on the Seminary's doorstep.

Resolved, That this Convention hears with pleasure of the training of women missionaries, being furnished by the Southern Baptist Theological Seminary; and while approving and commending the work already being done, the Convention respectfully recommends to the Seminary Faculty and Trustees, the further enlargement and better equipment of this department as the needs may demand and as the means in hand may justify, and earnestly hopes that our people shall give this important work their earnest sympathy and support.[21]

"The resolution from Dr. Frost calling for the perfecting of this Seminary training school for women missionaries was adopted." [22]

Progress was slow, but the courage of the women in asking for the appointment of a joint committee to consider the whole question brought them one step nearer their goal—a school for training women under the sponsorship of Woman's Missionary Union.

Gaining Momentum

These resolutions in both bodies aroused unusual interest throughout the denomination, and as a result of the publicity there was quite an increase in attendance of women at the Seminary during the 1903–1904 session. Dr. Mullins reported toward the end of the school year, "Forty-eight women have attended lectures regularly, ten of whom expect to be missionaries and others active Christian workers. The majority of the whole number are wives of the students." [23]

Dr. Mullins also reported that through the gift of a Christian woman of Louisville, Miss Beulah D. Fuller, the Seminary was able to add a special training class in practical mission methods for women. The faculty, as a matter of course, asked the young missions professor to teach this class. And so began Dr. Carver's close, formal connection with the school as the first special teacher for women. Among the men of that period who were sincerely interested in the movement none worked harder to promote the beginning of a training school than did Dr. Carver. In the providence of God he alone of his generation was spared to be the friend and adviser of its management and the teacher of its hundreds of students through fifty years.

A Home for the Ladies

The failure of the joint committee to present a positive program of action to Woman's Missionary Union and the Southern Baptist Convention at their annual meetings in 1904 did not discourage Dr. Mullins and his faculty. They believed that the training school was needed, and they now had the evidence that the majority of the leadership in the denomination were of the same mind. They moved along in the faith that the difficulties would be overcome in due time.

They outlined a two-year course of study for women and encouraged them through denominational papers to enrol in the Woman's Training Department of the Seminary. The article explained that board could be secured in the neighborhood of the Seminary at prices ranging from three to five dollars a week. In conclusion Dr. Mullins said, "We hope at a later date to have a home for the ladies who come as students in charge of a matron. The Baptist women of Kentucky and many women from other states are much interested in this enterprise, and will doubtless provide this home in the near future." [24]

This "home for the ladies" perhaps materialized even earlier than Dr. Mullins anticipated. At the annual meeting of the Kentucky Baptist women in June, 1904, Dr. Mullins was asked to present the "cause of the Woman's Missionary Training School." Miss Eliza Broadus, chairman of the Central Committee of Kentucky, reported that "the Woman's Missionary Association of Kentucky in its recent meeting heartily endorsed the movement to furnish the home that is urgently needed, and promised to collect funds toward the purpose." Typical of the way Kentucky women responded to this appeal was the action of the women of the Long Run Association. At their annual meeting in September the women met in a tent while the men held their session in the church, and "a contribution was made for the Woman's Training School in connection with the Seminary." [25]

At the opening of the 1904 session four girls found their way to Louisville to enter the Seminary's training school. Feeling timid and lonely in this man's world, they naturally gravitated together and soon found a room that they could rent from a Seminary couple, Mr. and Mrs. J. H. Moore. In an orderly fashion they used one corner as the kitchen, another as a dressing room, and the other two as bedrooms. The sitting room was around the open grate, and the study table in the center of the room.

The young missions professor, Dr. Carver, who was again teaching the practical missions course for women, discussed the plight of these girls with Mrs. Carver and other faculty wives. Miss Broadus, eldest daughter of the noted second president of the Seminary, was asked to take the initiative in working out a better plan for the living arrangements of the four girls. After conference with various Louisville Baptist women, she called a meeting of representative women from the Baptist churches of the city.

About twenty women attended this meeting, held at Walnut Street Baptist Church. Miss Broadus wisely asked Mrs. S. E. Woody to preside. This able and energetic young woman from Texas had recently come to the city as the bride of a promising young physician. Mrs. W. J. McGlothlin, wife of the professor of church history at the Seminary, was called on to explain the purpose of the meeting: to consider the question of providing a home for the young women attending Seminary classes. Following a lively discussion, this small band of women committed themselves to the task. There was no time to be lost since four girls who needed the protection and the supervision of a home were already on hand.

Officers were elected to proceed with the project: Mrs. Woody serving as chairman, Mrs. George B. Eager, as vice-chairman, Mrs. McGlothlin, as treasurer, and Miss Fannie Moses, as secretary. By February this committee, or board of managers, as they began to call themselves, numbered nineteen, one member from each Baptist church in Louisville.

The officers, under Mrs. Woody's aggressive leadership, located a two-story house on South Fourth Street, a few blocks from the Seminary, and furnished it with odds and ends of furniture and equipment contributed by Louisville Baptists. Mrs. Ann Weigal, a widow and a member of East Baptist Church, was secured as matron and house mother. She and her two young daughters, Linda and Nancy, moved in at once to make ready for the four pioneers, Clemmie Ford of Tennessee, Rena Groover of Georgia, Alice Huey of Alabama, and Ella Jeter of Oklahoma. They moved in on the day before Thanksgiving and had their first meal together on Thanksgiving Day, November 26, 1904.

As one of the four, Miss Alice Huey, in a talk to a group of women in her state, told something of the experiences of that year.

> Students of the Seminary began to tell their people about us and many good things came to us from the country, especially from churches of Brothers Cannedy and Howerton. . . .
> Highland Church [in Louisville] gave many things to the Home . . .
> Even the young men of New York Hall [the Seminary dormitory] caught the inspiration and gave us a hall tree.

The churches gave one house warming after another, each trying to see how liberal it could be, each pastor leaving a benediction on the home.[26]

Shortly after this original group was settled, the young, city missionary, Miss Emma Leachman, moved in as a boarder to share their home life and fellowship. She had sat in on the Seminary classes from time to time, so she had much in common with these girls. The relationship established at this time continued until 1921 when Miss Leachman went to the Home Mission Board as a field worker. Her influence through these formative years cannot be estimated. There were always some students who loved her devotedly and some who feared her, but whether they loved or feared her, they all admired her and remembered her with growing appreciation as they tried to put into practice what they had learned from her.

By February seven other girls from Tennessee, Texas, Oklahoma, and Kentucky were admitted, taxing the capacity of the small house. But these resourceful girls were too grateful for their own opportunities to refuse to surrender some of their comforts so that the new students might share with them the blessings of study in a homelike atmosphere. There was the attic! They had discovered it at the recent Christmas party. What did it matter if they could not stand straight except in the center of the room? Three of the boarders cleaned the new-found quarters and cheerfully vacated the second floor to make room for the new girls.

With rare faith and courage, the Louisville women met the emergency and kept the little home going from month to month. With no cash in hand, in fact, nothing but promises from a small band of women, they rented a house at forty dollars a month. Mrs. Woody took personal responsibility for the rent and the utilities. These valiant women exercised the sort of faith that removed their mountain of difficulty. When the treasury was empty they prayed together, and their needs were met as the little gifts came in from Kentucky women and occasionally from other states.

The Larger Vision

The Louisville women provided the home as a temporary measure to meet an emergency. From the beginning, however, they prayed and planned for something permanent and far-reaching to emerge out of their effort. Mrs. McGlothlin expressed their aspirations in a report at the end of the first year in these words: "There is a larger vision which we are hoping and praying that we may see realized some day. It is the vision of a fully equipped training school for young women, equal to the best and under the control and direction of the Baptist women of the South." [27]

In the light of the larger vision they met the daily problems. The need was so urgent that they could not believe that Woman's Missionary Union would vote against an opportunity at the next annual meeting to take over a going missionary project. They did not wait idly, depending on God to do what they could do. Well in advance of the 1905 meeting, therefore, they got busy on a plan to bring the school before the women. During the spring months articles written by Mrs. Eager and Mrs. McGlothlin appeared in the state Baptist papers. These gifted writers reviewed the work of the home during its first year, outlined the needs for the immediate future, and appealed for help from the "Baptist sisterhood of the South."

As they planned their course of action, the Louisville women realized that the most important step in getting the young school before Woman's Missionary Union was to get a place on the prepared program for the forthcoming annual meeting. At this point they faced their most difficult problem. They were evidently afraid to approach Miss Armstrong, who must have had the major responsibility in preparing the annual meeting programs. Mrs. Woody, in explaining the procedure of the local group, said,

24

After the report of the joint committee of W.M.U. and S.B.C. had been adopted at Nashville, the attitude of the Cor. Sec. of W.M.U. towards the whole matter was such that the committee here felt that it might be an embarrassment to open the subject except with the Pres. of the W.M.U. . . . . It would have been painful to have proceeded against the expressed disapproval of our Corresponding Secretary.[28]

As a result they by-passed the corresponding secretary and wrote directly to the vice-presidents in the states, asking them to use their influence in getting the school before the Union at the forthcoming annual meeting in Kansas City, Missouri. To strengthen their case with the Union, they appealed to the boards of the Convention, asking them to recommend to the women in session the encouragement and support of the training school.

The Crisis at Kansas City

Out of this muddled situation it was inevitable that a great deal of feeling should be generated. By this time, the issue of the school had practically become a tug of war between Miss Armstrong and the WMU Executive Committee in Baltimore on one side and the majority of the leadership of the Convention on the other. Perhaps Miss Armstrong thought that her clever disposition in the joint committee of the troublesome issue the year before had settled it for all time as far as the Union was concerned.

However, Dr. Mullins did not consider it settled and sought to reopen the irritating subject. At the meeting of the WMU Executive Committee in Baltimore in October, 1904, the record states that "some letters from Dr. Mullins were read on the subject of the Training School for women." The reader is left to wonder whether the letters were acknowledged or ignored.

When the annual meeting opened in Kansas City, the atmosphere was heavy with tension and misunderstanding. Mrs. Eager and Mrs. Woody were among the Kentucky delegates, prepared to speak on their beloved project if the opportunity was given them.

In the opening session Miss M. Gibson, president of Scarritt Bible and Training School, was present as the official representative of the Methodist foreign and home mission boards. She was introduced, spoke briefly, and invited the Union to visit the Scarritt Training School. Here was the opportunity to see a successful school, dating back to 1892. To the friends of the movement this opening session must have seemed auspicious. At any rate, something inspired expression and action. Mrs. J. L. Burnham, of Missouri, offered the following resolution: "*Resolved* that the W.M.U. endorse the Home for the young women attending the Woman's Missionary Training School in Louisville, and heartily commend the Home to the sympathy and help of State Central Committees." [29]

Miss Armstrong rose quickly and moved that the resolution be tabled until half-past three that afternoon and asked the privilege of speaking on the resolution at that time. The situation which she had feared and tried so valiantly to block had now gotten out of hand.

Mrs. Woody, quick to take advantage of an opportunity, asked that Dr. Mullins also be allowed the privilege of speaking to the resolution. Miss Armstrong waived the right to speak first and granted that privilege to Dr. Mullins. Mrs. Eager and Mrs. Woody extended to Dr. Mullins the invitation to be present at the afternoon session as their spokesman.

Dr. Mullins had carefully prepared for just such an occasion. He knew that under the circumstances open discussion of the training school was bound to come in the meeting of the Seminary Board of Trustees, on the Convention platform, and in the WMU sessions. As a part of his preparation he wrote a "Statement of Facts" at the request of the Seminary faculty. This statement was presented to the Board of Trustees at their annual meeting. The board adopted the statement with only minor changes. Dr. W. W. Landrum, one of the leading pastors of the denomination, was appointed chairman of a special committee to go to the woman's meeting in an effort to explain the Seminary's position.

When the afternoon session opened, the house was crowded with delegates and visitors, for by now it was no secret that important decisions would be made at this session. According to plan, the special order was called for and Dr. Mullins, tall, stately, poised, impressive, was introduced. He in turn presented the gracious, beloved, and trusted Dr. Landrum, who read detailed recommendations from the Board of Trustees.

Dr. Landrum tried valiantly not only to clarify the misunderstanding regarding the way the Woman's Training Department of the Seminary had been started but also to support the Louisville women in their effort to lead Woman's Missionary Union to adopt the home which had been opened for women students at the Seminary. He reviewed the action of the Board of Trustees in admitting to classes women preparing for mission work because no school for women was in existence in the South. He further explained that the Seminary had never planned to do anything more than to place at the disposal of women students all the privileges and advantages for training already in existence at the Seminary.

In conclusion he came directly to the major reason for the appointment of the special committee to appear before Woman's Missionary Union:

It is our firm conviction that the time has come when the work of training our Baptist women for mission and Christian work should have the support of our Baptist women generally. Our Louisville sisters have made an excellent beginning, and we send out this statement in their behalf, and ask for them the sympathy and co-operation and financial assistance of the Baptist Woman's Missionary Union, and our Baptist women all over the South.[30]

When Dr. Landrum finished, Dr. Mullins spoke briefly. He explained that women had been attending Seminary classes for several years. The majority of them planned to do special Christian work at home or in foreign lands. The increasing numbers year by year had created the problem. They needed a home where they could live at small expense and at the same time be surrounded by home influences.

The report of this meeting that was printed in the *Christian Index* closed with these words: "After discussion of some length, participated in by Miss A. W. Armstrong, Mrs. J. H. Eager, Mrs. W. D. Chipley and others, the vote was taken, and the resolution was lost." [31]

Mrs. George B. Eager threw more light on the final vote in her report in the *Baptist Argus.* After Dr. Mullins and Dr. Landrum had spoken,

Miss Armstrong then reviewed the subject from its beginning, and frankly stated her thorough disapproval of the work in its present state and of the methods of the Louisville women in bringing it before the Southern women, the impression of disloyalty to the officers of the Union having been made. This feeling the President [Mrs. John A. Barker] shared. Mrs. W. D. Chipley, of Florida, made a noble defense of the Kentucky women, and Mrs. George B. Eager was granted the opportunity to speak for the [Louisville] Executive Committee. She expressed the sincere regret of the committee that anything they had said or done had so impressed the leaders of the Union and heartily assured them that only deep interest in the work that God had laid at the doors of Louisville women had entered into any of their efforts. She was followed by Miss Armstrong and others. The vote was taken and stood at 22 for the home, 25 against it.[32]

How can the failure of the resolution to pass be explained? The resonant voice and dignified bearing of Dr. Landrum must have added weight to the clear recommendations from the Board of Trustees. The forceful and logical expression of the great Dr. Mullins must have been convincing. There is but one answer. There was a third powerful personality in that meeting that afternoon, and she was opposed to what the men were advocating with all the force of her being. Her contemporaries often spoke of her as the "indomitable Miss Armstrong," and indomitable she was! The more the Louisville group tried to enlist the co-operation of the Union, the more determined she was that they should not.

The women in that meeting must have been very much confused. To many of them Miss Armstrong *was* the Union. She had been their secretary since the Union was organized, serving without salary. She had refused a salary more than once, though the secretaries of the boards and the WMU leaders urged her to accept it. The women loved her, and they believed in her. Some felt that whatever position she took on any matter must be right, so they voted with her.

There were others who, in spite of their respect for Miss Armstrong's leadership, dared to think for themselves and vote according to their convictions. There was a third group who did not vote at all. They may have hesitated to vote against their secretary, but they must have begun to wonder who was right and so remained neutral.

Mrs. Eager often told the story of this meeting in her inimitable fashion. She said, "Miss Armstrong became so angry that she did not address Dr. Mullins as 'Dr.,' nor did she make him plural! She called him 'Mr. Mullin!'"

The Kentucky delegation was very much discouraged by the unexpected outcome of the discussion. They had pinned their hopes on Dr. Mullins. Unbelievable as it was, he had failed by three votes to get the resolution passed. They now felt that theirs was a lost cause. Some of the other women were more optimistic. Victory was in sight. The friends of the movement had come to the firm conviction that something constructive and progressive should be done before adjournment. The next day, therefore, Mrs. W. F. Elliott, of Missouri, offered the following resolution, which was adopted without discussion:

Resolved, That we recommend to the prayerful investigation of our sisters all over the Southland, the work now being done at the

Theological Seminary at Louisville, and the desirability of sustaining a home for the young women who may avail themselves of the training offered, in order that we may be prepared to decide at our next meeting whether the W.M.U. shall undertake the work of sustaining the Home.

Resolved, That we hereby express our appreciation of the generosity of our sisters of Kentucky, in the work they have done in providing a home for those young women who have already been in training at the Seminary, and recommend that all sisters who feel that the object is worthy, render such assistance as they may be able.[33]

Miss Armstrong did not raise her voice against this resolution. She knew that she was defeated. Before the session was over she announced that she would not stand for re-election the following year. Mrs. J. A. Barker, president, and the members of the Executive Committee in Baltimore also made public their decision to sever their connection with the Union as officers at the next annual meeting.

In the closing words of her report of "W.M.U. in Kansas City," Mrs. Eager paid generous tribute to Miss Armstrong:

The same officers were nominated and unanimously elected. In accepting office, the president and corresponding secretary both announced their unalterable decision not to serve after this year. Great appreciation is felt and expressed for the valuable services of these two officers.

The corresponding secretary has for seventeen years laid her great talents and her time and strength ungrudgingly upon the altar of service and has as a reward seen the work swing into an orbit wider than hope or thought ever pictured. Southern Baptists value most highly the remarkable work of this remarkable woman.[34]

The Southern Baptist Convention took due notice of the effort to get the young school endorsed and added its approval in the following resolution, which was passed unanimously:

Resolved, That this convention recognizes with pleasure the work done by the Louisville Baptist women in support of the Training School and in the maintenance of the home for women workers attending the Seminary in Louisville. We also rejoice in the recent action of the Woman's Missionary Union favorable to this noble enterprise, and most heartily commend the Home and Training School to the sympathy and support of all our Baptist people, and especially to our Baptist women.[35]

They Were Not Alone

The Louisville women's spirits were lifted by the general demonstration of interest in their beloved project. They were disappointed, of course, that the Union did not adopt the school, but they were encouraged to believe that this step would be taken at the next annual meeting.

Back in Louisville, the women faced their work with renewed hope and courage. The first task was to find a larger house. Correspondence during the spring had indicated that there might be as many as twenty-five students for the next session. The Fourth Street house had been filled to capacity with only eleven girls the year before. In due time they found a house that was admirably suited to their needs, the Dulaney mansion, located at Eighth and Broadway, four blocks west of the Seminary. It was described as one of the handsomest of the old homes in Louisville, for years the residence of one of the city's wealthiest families.

The larger house would be more expensive to maintain, so Mrs. Woody began sending out calls for help through the state Baptist papers and in direct letters to the central committees. She later reported that timely help came from Kentucky, Alabama, Missouri, North Carolina, South Carolina, Florida, Georgia, Tennessee, Texas, Virginia, Mississippi, and Arkansas.

By faith and prayer the Louisville women carried on during the year. They often told in later years of meeting during the early weeks of that session to make rag rugs for the cold, rough floors of the old mansion. Before they left, Mrs. Woody would

31

bring the mounting bills and Mrs. Eager would take over. Down on their knees they would go in earnest prayer for guidance and help. In due time the contributions came in to tide them over from month to month. What a wonderful feeling it was to know that now they were not alone. God seemed to be putting approval on the loved work. They thanked him and took courage.

A Tempest in Baltimore

While the tension was being eased in Louisville, it was mounting in Baltimore. Miss Armstrong and the WMU Executive Committee would have saved themselves a painful experience had they accepted the fact that what was done in Kansas City was done according to democratic procedures. Their unwillingness to abide by the decision of the majority put them on the defensive and embroiled them in a year of bitter rehashing of the whole story of the training school movement, dating back to 1900.

The committee met shortly after returning to Baltimore from Kansas City. Miss Alice Armstrong read a letter that had been prepared by her sister to go out to all central committees and state papers. There is a clue to the contents of this letter in the WMU column of the *Baptist and Reflector* for June 15, 1905. Mention was made there of an official letter from Miss Armstrong in which she stated that for reasons unnecessary to give she had given notice in Kansas City that she would terminate her work as corresponding secretary at the end of the Convention year in May, 1906.

After the letter was read the committee then endorsed the following "Official Action of the Executive Committee," which was to go out with the letter:

At a session of the Executive Committee, W.M.U., held Thursday, May 25, in Baltimore, a very careful review was made of the history of the movement to establish a Woman's Missionary Training School in connection with the Theological Seminary, Louisville, Ky., from its inception, in 1900, by Rev. E. Z. Simmons, returned missionary from China, to its presentation, with Home for Students, to Woman's Missionary Union in Kansas City, Mo. Official records, letters and recent actions preceding and during the meetings in Kansas City were in evidence.

By unanimous vote, the Executive Committee endorsed the attitude of the President and the Corresponding Secretary at annual meeting, toward the Training School and Home at Louisville, and recognized their devotion to the work by remaining in office till the close of the present Conventional year, May, 1906.

The Executive Committee will decline renomination.[36]

At the October meeting of the Executive Committee letters from Dr. Willingham, Dr. Frost, and Miss Broadus and clippings from the *Christian Index* were read. Dr. T. P. Bell, editor of the *Index*, had expressed himself rather frankly, to put it mildly, on Miss Armstrong's attitude toward the training school. The reading of Dr. Bell's article resulted in a motion that a letter should be written to all state papers "expressing their indignation at the shameful persecution to which the Corresponding Secretary is being subjected by Dr. T. P. Bell." [37]

The next item of business was a "Statement and Protest" in which they put themselves

On record as according entirely with the attitude of the President, Mrs. J. A. Barker, and the Secretary, Miss Annie W. Armstrong, in opposing the Training School for Women at the Theological Seminary in Louisville and the Home for Women Students established by the women of Louisville. This attitude represented the support of two principles: the Scriptural position that women are not to preach, involving the corollary of being taught to preach, as the Seminary course for students is intended to do. Also, that Christian work must be done by right methods, involving condemnation of the methods by which the support of the Home for Women Students in Louisville has been urged upon Woman's Missionary Union.

It will be remembered that both the officers declined reelection. They consented, however, to serve for one year that time might be allowed to prepare for needed changes so that harm should not come to the work. It might be supposed that this generous decision to remain in office when both earnestly desired to retire, would have been universally appreciated and respected. But there are those in control of the Biblical Recorder, N. C., and the Christian Index, Ga., who are using this eighteenth year of gratuitous service as an opportunity, and the Secretary, Miss Armstrong, as a target for criticism that is unreasonable, ungentlemanly and unChristian. The aim is to injure the Secretary in the opinion of the public and to discredit Woman's Missionary Union methods of work. The long years of faithful unremitting service and the very substantial success of Woman's Missionary Union efforts will, doubtless, be a convincing reply to unworthy criticism.

But the Executive Committee is unwilling to be silent at this juncture and desires to be understood as reprobating newspaper criticism which is misrepresentative of facts, unkind in spirit, and has assumed the character of persecution of an individual.[38]

After the approval of the "Statement and Protest," which was sent to the secretaries of the three boards and to the chairmen of the state central committees, letters were read from the secretaries of the three boards, the central committees of Texas and Arkansas, Miss Broadus, and Mrs. E. Y. Mullins. The record of this important meeting adds another note: "A letter from Professor Carver of Louisville Seminary was read on same subject. Will be placed on file and Professor Carver so notified by Corresponding Secretary."

Miss Armstrong reported that the Central Committee of Georgia had endorsed the action of the Woman's Missionary Union Executive Committee and that the Executive Committee of Virginia had appointed "a committee of seven to investigate this matter of a Home for female missionaries at Louisville, Ky., and report back to Executive Committee [of Virginia] after annual meeting."

Dr. Carver, as secretary of the Seminary faculty, continued to write to Miss Armstrong in spite of her efforts to ignore him. About the February meeting of the WMU Executive Committee the record says, the "Corresponding Secretary read a communication from Professor W. O. Carver of Louisville Seminary, and Miss Amstrong moved that no notice be taken of

34

Dr. Carver's letters, but that they be placed on file. After considerable discussion, motion carried." [39]

Among the many letters read at that meeting, the most devastating in its effect was one from Dr. Mullins asking that the Executive Committee correct an incorrect statement in the "Protest." It was evident by this time that some members of the Executive Committee were beginning to think for themselves. When Mrs. James F. Tyler made a motion that Dr. Mullins' letter be placed on file, five members dared to vote against it. It now was apparent that they had reluctantly agreed to ignore Dr. Carver's letters, but their sense of courtesy would not let them so treat a letter from the president of the Seminary. Mrs. W. C. Lowndes then moved that they reconsider the "Protest," and the same five women voted with her. With the committee now clearly divided, Mrs. Lowndes claimed the privilege of a minority report.

At the next meeting of the committee the main business was the reconsideration of the "Protest" and the adoption of the majority and minority reports. The majority report read as follows:

Whereas; A Theological Seminary has separate existence from schools and colleges for the single purpose of teaching its students to preach;

And Whereas: Every study converges toward this point; therefore, all students pursuing this course, in whole or in part, are taught to preach. This is a self-evident proposition.

Whereas, the study of Homiletics, defined in the Seminary's catalogue as "Homiletics, or preparation and delivery of sermons," is "not recommended for the woman's course"; yet, Mrs. H. H. Steinmetz is entered in the class of Homiletics, in the catalogue of 1902–03, as having attended this class regularly

Therefore, be it resolved: That the injury to the Seminary does not lie in the statement of the self-evident proposition that the Seminary course of study is intended to teach its students to preach; nor does the remedy for the injury lie in withdrawing the language of the self-evident proposition. The remedy lies in withdrawing the women students from the Seminary.

Resolved: That the undersigned reaffirm the declarations contained in the original "statement."[40]

This report was signed by Mrs. J. A. Barker, president; Mrs. J. F. Tyler, vice-president; Annie W. Armstrong, corresponding secretary; Ella V. Ricker, treasurer; Alice Armstrong; Mrs. M. B. Brown; and Mrs. R. B. Kelley.

The minority report read as follows:

We, the undersigned, constituting a minority of the Executive Committee Woman's Missionary Union, who voted at the meeting March 20, 1906, to correct the statement in Circular letter sent out by the Executive Committee October 10, 1905, regarding the Training School for Young Women Students at Louisville Seminary do hereby state that when said letter was written we believed that young women attending said Training School were being taught to preach.

Since then, however, information has come to our knowledge which leads us to believe that said action was taken without having all the facts necessary to a full understanding of the matter, and as the statement is now positively denied by the President and Faculty of the Seminary and by the President of the Board of Trustees, we regret having made such a statement, and desire now to correct it by withdrawing same.[41]

This report was signed by Clara M. Woolford, chairman, Mrs. A. C. Johnson, Mrs. W. R. Nimmo, Mrs. W. C. Lowndes, Mrs. A. J. Clark, and Mrs. Helen M. Grady.

It was voted to send copies of the two reports to the president of the Board of Trustees and the president of the Seminary, the state central committees, and the secretaries of the three boards.

At a former meeting the entire committee had voted to stand by the president and the corresponding secretary by declining to serve after May, 1906. At this time, however, five members signified their willingness to serve again on the Executive Committee if the Woman's Missionary Union so desired; they were Mrs. Johnson, Mrs. Clark, Mrs. Lowndes, Mrs. Nimmo, and Miss Woolford.

Within a year the fellowship of a close-knit group of Christian workers was broken, and its members came to a definite parting of the ways. It is remembered with gratitude that the names Lowndes, Johnson, Nimmo, and Woolford are found in the records of Woman's Missionary Union as active and valuable workers to the end of their lives. They became, also, staunch friends of the Woman's Missionary Union Training School after its adoption by the Union. As to the others, it is well to remember that they voted according to their convictions.

Foiled by the Constitution

The friends of the training school movement went to Chattanooga in early May, 1906, with confidence that the major problems had apparently been solved. The resolution passed the year before had prepared the way for the question to be decided at this annual meeting. The response of the women during the year had indicated that the majority would vote for the adoption of the school. Accordingly, when the first session was called to order by the president, Mrs. J. A. Barker, on the morning of May 10, many visitors, as well as delegates, were in the audience.

There was an atmosphere of suspense and excited interest in the crowd. No one would accuse men of being curious about what goes on in a woman's organization, but they were there in large numbers. The *Christian Index* reported that so many brethren came to the meeting that the president had repeatedly to ask the gentlemen to retire, as this was a woman's meeting.

It is easy to understand the curiosity of delegates and visitors, including the men. Two matters of consuming interest were on the agenda—the final report of Miss Armstrong and the decision about the training school in Louisville. What would the corresponding secretary say as she bowed out of the Union? What would be done about the proposed school which had been the bone of contention for six years?

At the first session Miss Armstrong submitted her report, a detailed review of the work of the WMU since its organization in 1888. She carefully avoided any mention of the issue that had consumed her interest and dissipated her influence during the last years of her term of service.

It was a bit ironical that the unfinished business regarding the training school was taken up at the same session. "Mrs. W. S. Leake, Va., offered a Resolution in reference to establishing a Training School for women missionaries in Louisville, Ky." Mrs. F. S. Davis, of Texas, moved that consideration be postponed until the afternoon session. Another motion granted to Mrs. George B. Eager the privilege of speaking first on the question.

At the afternoon session Mrs. Eager introduced the discussion by reading a communication from the Board of Trustees of the Seminary, endorsing the movement and offering hearty co-operation with the women in carrying on the work of the training school. Following Mrs. Eager, a charming young woman from North Carolina, Miss Fannie E. S. Heck, who was destined to play a vital part in the development of the school during its formative years, took the floor. Other speakers included such well-known leaders as Mrs. W. S. Leake, of Virginia; Mrs. J. B. Gambrell, of Texas; Mrs. A. C. Johnson, of Maryland; Mrs. C. A. Stakely, of Alabama; Mrs. S. E. Woody, of Kentucky; and Mrs. Charles S. Gardner, of Virginia. With such an array of speakers, it is easy to understand the report that "consideration of sustaining the home brought about a long and breezy discussion."

Someone finally decided that enough had been said and called for the question. To the dismay of friends of the movement, the president ruled that, according to the constitution, a new work could not be undertaken without previous notice of three months to the Woman's Missionary Union, save by a unanimous vote of the body. When the vote was taken, there was an overwhelming majority vote for the resolution, but with the help of the constitution the opposition won the victory.

Perhaps this was the deep darkness before the dawn that would usher in a new day. The gifted and respected Miss Heck was elected president of Woman's Missionary Union for the third time, and she was a friend of the movement. The "indomitable Miss Armstrong," the leader of the opposition, was leaving the ranks of the Union.

At a later session Mrs. A. J. Wheeler, of Tennessee, offered the following resolution, which was adopted:

In view of the generous offer received from the Trustees of the Seminary and the Committee on the Home in Louisville

Resolved, That we have heard with gratification concerning the success of the work done at the Theological Seminary at Louisville, Ky., for the young women who are preparing themselves for missionary labors, and have received with pleasure the request from the Seminary Trustees for the co-operation of the W.M.U. in aid of this important work.

Resolved further, That the thanks of the Union be tendered the sisters from the States which have so cordially aided in the maintenance of the Home for these young women during the past year, and that we commend this object to the ever increasing generosity of the women and the societies of our entire constituency.

Resolved, That a Committee of one from each State be appointed to consider the advisability of establishing a Woman's Missionary Training School in Louisville as soon as the constitution will admit of it.[42]

As usual, there was no lack of women to speak on this ever-recurring subject. This time, however, all were in favor of establishing a school—all except Miss Armstrong, who had a final word against it.

Dear Miss Armstrong! She could not be convinced against

her will. Strangely enough, the expression from the body regarding her retirement seemed to come as an afterthought. Following the report of the nominating committee and the election of officers, Mrs. J. W. Vesey, of Alabama, moved

That an expression of appreciation be made by a rising vote of the W.M.U. to our retiring President, Mrs. J. A. Barker, for her efficient work and untiring efforts during the past few years.

Mrs. A. J. Wheeler, asked for a moment of silent prayer for the retiring corresponding secretary, closed by one verse of "God be with you."

At the last session Mrs. Burnham, of Missouri, offered a resolution "that our gratitude be expressed in a rising vote of thanks to Miss Armstrong, our retiring Cor. Sec. for her 18 years of service in our work." [43]

If the group failed in any way to express appreciation to Miss Armstrong as she left the work, Woman's Missionary Union tried to make amends in 1933 by naming the home mission offering, which she had started in 1895, the "Annie Armstrong Offering." Again, in 1938, when the Golden Jubilee of Woman's Missionary Union was being celebrated, she was honored in many ways. An old woman at that time, living in retirement in Baltimore, she seemed pleased when an official committee visited her, bringing greetings from the Union. In the conversation she showed that the old wound was healed by asking, "How is the Training School getting along?"

Faith Takes the Final Step

Immediately following the close of the annual meeting in Chattanooga, Miss Heck, the new president, called the Executive Committee together. At this time she announced the special committee which had been authorized to consider the advisability of establishing a woman's missionary training school in Louisville. She gave necessary instructions to the committee, then left the matter with them.

Mrs. Eager and Mrs. Woody returned to Louisville, disappointed but not discouraged. They were growing a disciplined faith in the hard school of delay and frustration. Now that a Southwide committee had been appointed by a president who was openly in favor of the school, they had every reason to believe that success was in sight.

Back in Louisville the faithful group of women were faced with the problem of planning for another year of operating the home in faith, so there was not much time left for needless worry. They rented the old Dulaney mansion again and secured a superintendent for the home, Mrs. C. M. V. Follette from North Carolina. A music teacher and a housekeeper were added to the staff. A course of medical lectures, given by some of the city's most prominent physicians, was included in the curriculum. Mrs. Woody sent out appeals for help through the state papers, asking the "missionary societies to consider this needy and important work and send contributions." Faith and work brought them through the year without debt.

In the fall of that year Dr. Mullins began the custom of inviting the staff and students of the home to Thanksgiving dinner in the Seminary dining hall. This delightful courtesy was continued until the Seminary and training school groups became too large to be accommodated in the limited quarters.

While the Board of Managers in Louisville was meeting usual problems and some new ones as well, the Woman's Missionary Union Executive Committee in Baltimore was functioning smoothly under Miss Heck's direction. No one had yet been found to succeed Miss Armstrong. No mention was made of the training school until the March meeting. The record of that meeting states:

Miss Heck read a letter from Mrs. George B. Eager concerning the Baptist Woman's Missionary Training School Home at Louisville. Resolutions by Executive Committee on the acceptance of the "Home" by Woman's Missionary Union were read and adopted unanimously by ballot. A copy of these resolutions are to be sent to the Board of Managers of the Training School Home.[44]

Again, at the April meeting of this committee a letter was read from Mrs. Eager regarding the school. Dr. Mullins also wrote Miss Heck giving practical suggestions as to the wording of the provisional resolutions of the Executive Committee. Mrs. J. H. Eager was appointed by Miss Heck to be chairman of a special committee to draft the resolutions in accordance with Dr. Mullins' suggestions.

The historic nineteenth session of Woman's Missionary Union met in Richmond, May 16–19, 1907. Due notice having been given of the proposed change in the constitution, the necessary amendment opening the way for the Union to take over the Training School and home in Louisville was offered. It was reported that quite a spirited discussion followed. Finally, time ran out and there was a call for the question, with ninety voting for and two against the resolution.

The next day Mrs. F. S. Davis, of Texas, stated that having received additional information, she would move that the vote on said amendment be made unanimous. Mrs. J. B. Gambrell, of Texas, seconded the motion, and a rising vote was taken, making the action unanimous.

Immediately following the action clearing the way for the Union to take over the school, Mrs. George B. Eager moved that the following telegram of greeting be sent to Miss Armstrong: "By unanimous vote the Woman's Missionary Union herewith expresses to you its grateful remembrance and appreciation for the valuable service you rendered in founding and establishing its work."

The Board of Trustees of the Seminary, through Dr. Mullins, surrendered to the Union the entire management and control of the woman's training school and offered all the advantages of the Seminary classes. The temporary Board of Managers offered the furnishings and equipment which they had collected, valued at $900.

Additional resolutions from the Executive Committee provided for the Union to "establish a Missionary Training School

in Louisville" to be called "Woman's Missionary Union Training School." Its management was to be in the hands of a general board of managers, a local board of managers, and an
advisory board of seven members, composed of two men connected with the Seminary, two Baptist laymen of Louisville,
and the secretaries of the Foreign and Home Mission boards
and the Sunday School Board. These boards were to be elected
annually by Woman's Missionary Union.

A special committee was appointed to make all arrangements for the opening of the school—find a suitable building,
set up entrance requirements, draft the curriculum, find necessary instructors, prepare and issue a catalogue—a large order
for a brief summer.

At the final session of the 1907 annual meeting Miss Heck
announced that the Southern Baptist Convention had taken
up an offering for the needed building in Louisville amounting to $4,700. After prayer by Mrs. Leake, of Virginia, and a
plea by Mrs. Eager, of Baltimore, the women took an offering
which reached the amazing figure of $10,129.81.

A new day had come to Woman's Missionary Union. A great
new missionary venture had been undertaken on faith. After
years of consideration, debate, and division, the Union was
now adopting with enthusiasm a project that would be lovingly
supported for the next fifty years. Two great building programs
would be launched and carried through to completion without
debt, and hundreds of choice young women would be trained
for service at home and abroad.

Those pioneer women of 1907 began a pilgrimage of faith
that leads on into the future. There has been no lack of follow-
ers through the years. They had convictions about the needs of
their day which they translated into action. Pioneers are still
needed today—pioneers with convictions about today's needs
and opportunities, pioneers who will continue to build on the
foundations laid by faith fifty years ago.

2

A Decade of Growth

We should so live and labor in our time that
what came to us as seed may go to the next generation as blossom, and what came to us as
blossom may go to them as fruit.—This is what
we mean by progress.—H. W. Beecher

In the providence of God the Woman's Missionary Union
Training School began its work under favorable conditions.
The year of 1907 was a year of great missionary fervor. The
centennial of missions in China was being celebrated throughout the Christian world. Many Southern Baptists attended the
China Centenary Missionary Conference in Shanghai and
came home to share their new zeal for world missions.

One of the direct results of the centennial was the promotion
of the Layman's Missionary Movement in this country. While
Woman's Missionary Union was holding the final session of its
annual meeting in Richmond and taking the offering for the
building of the new Training School, a mass meeting was being held in another auditorium for the purpose of organizing
a Southern Baptist unit of the Layman's Movement.

Another missionary influence in America at this time, especially among college students, was the Haystack Centennial,
commemorating one of the most far-reaching prayer meetings
ever held. In 1806 a small group of students in Williams College took refuge under a haystack during a thunder storm and
there pledged themselves in prayer to the evangelization of
Asia. One hundred years later their influence and example were

still leading other college men and women to dedicate themselves to the same great task of proclaiming the gospel to the
whole world.

The Training School was fortunate to come into being at a
time of unusual denominational unity. The Baptist World Alliance had just been organized, and the first World Congress had
been held in London in the summer of 1906. The fellowship
and inspiration of that meeting had perhaps given Baptists
the greatest impetus to participation in world missions since the
organization of the first Baptist Missionary Society in Kettering, England, in 1792.

These worldwide missionary influences were making a definite impact on the plans and program of Woman's Missionary
Union. The first mass meeting for missions held at the first
evening session of the 1907 meeting gave the women an unforgettable experience. The beloved Dr. R. J. Willingham, secretary of the Foreign Mission Board, presided. Dr. B. D. Gray,
Dr. J. M. Frost, and Dr. T. B. Ray spoke on phases of mission
work; Dr. E. F. Tatum told of the Centennial in China; a dozen
other missionaries from China, Japan, Africa, Panama, and the
Western frontier were presented. In this fashion the spirit was
created for a "venture of faith" not only in building for missions but also in giving to missions. Before these pioneer
women adjourned they had committed themselves to establish a
missionary training school, whose initial needs they had no
way of estimating; in addition, they had pledged to give
$100,000 to the Foreign Mission Board and $75,000 to the
Home Mission Board.

Again, in the providence of God the inauguration of this
school dedicated to missionary training took place on October 2, 1907, a day memorable in missionary history. On that
date in 1792 twelve unknown men met in Kettering, England,
and without fanfare organized the Baptist Society for Propa-
gating the Gospel Among the Heathen. More than a century
later something of their zeal, courage, and dedication made

October 2 mark the beginning of an epoch in world missions for Southern Baptists.

A Summer of Preparation

Mrs. Eager and Mrs. Woody returned to Louisville from the annual meeting in Chattanooga to share their victory with the local Board of Managers. They had been given a tremendous assignment for the summer, but it seemed light compared to the load they had carried for three years.

A special committee had been appointed to work out the plans for opening the school in the fall. Their first big problem was finding a suitable building. It must be near the Seminary and the cost within the maximum amount agreed on by the committee.

To help in this important search, Mr. T. H. Whayne, a leading real estate agent, had been named to the Advisory Committee. He soon found the building that seemed to meet every requirement—the Langham Apartment House on East Broadway, six blocks from the Seminary. It was in good repair, large enough to take care of fifty students, and suitable to the needs of the school with a minimum of changes.

When the owner learned for what purpose the building was to be used, he generously donated $2,500, leaving the sum to be paid at $20,500. The women had on hand for the building only the offerings taken in the Southern Baptist Convention and the Woman's Missionary Union, about $15,000, but after all, this was a "venture of faith."

The big order was finding a necessary staff, especially a principal. This title for the head of the school had been chosen, perhaps, for two reasons. This was the British term for the head of a school or college which had come into general use in this country. The second reason may have been the implications of the close relationship with the Seminary. At that stage, with the major part of the teaching to be done at the Seminary, it hardly seemed fitting to call the head of the school its president. Other similar schools at that time used the titles president, preceptress, and principal.

Miss Heck was chairman of the committee to secure a principal, with Mrs. Eager and Mrs. Woody sharing the responsibility with her. Mrs. Eager seemed to have a special gift for finding the right person for a given place. At this time she recalled an attractive young widow, Mrs. Maud Reynolds Mc-Lure, whom she had met in Alabama. Mrs. Eager had a growing impression that Mrs. McLure was the woman for the place. On investigation she learned that Mrs. McLure's young son was now in a boarding school and that she was teaching music at Cox College, Atlanta, Georgia.

To the first letter Mrs. McLure replied courteously that she was not fitted for such work. Mrs. Eager wrote again and again, each time receiving a similar answer. Finally, she decided to approach Mrs. McLure one more time, and if she still refused, the committee would consider the answer final.

By this time Mrs. McLure's resistance was wearing down, and she was beginning to wonder if God was calling her to this new and untried service. It so happened that young Tom Mc-Lure was at home for a visit, and before answering this latest urgent message she told him of the position that had been offered her. She added in a tone of finality, "But I cannot do it. I am not equipped for such a task."

Her son replied, "But you are, Mother. You can do it superbly." [1]

Not fully convinced, but with more faith in her own ability, she wired Mrs. Eager that she would at least consider the matter. Plans were worked out immediately for Miss Heck to meet Mrs. McLure for a conference in Greenville, South Carolina, at the Margaret Home. Miss Heck's persuasive presentation added to the call of God to Mrs. McLure's responsive soul gained an affirmative answer.

The special committee, which included Dr. Mullins, Dr. Carver, and Dr. Frost, then extended to her the official call at a salary of $75.00 per month plus living expenses in the school. She accepted without further question, set her affairs in order at Cox College, and went to Louisville promptly for conferences on plans for the opening. Since she had had no experience in this type of school, it was decided that she should go to Chicago for the month of September to study methods at the Baptist Missionary Training School, which had been in existence for twenty-six years.

Mrs. McLure's education had been the best that her day had to offer. In a brief biography published in 1940, her niece, Miss Hannah Reynolds, said, "As a child, private instructors taught her in the home, after which she attended school in Talladega, Alabama. Later she studied at Judson College, Marion, Alabama, and finally attended a finishing school in Baltimore."

Years later, Mrs. McLure sat in her living room at 334 East Broadway visiting with members of the staff. Looking across at a massive sofa that had been given to the school when the Margaret Home was closed in Greenville, she said, "How well I remember the day in the summer of 1907 when I sat on that sofa with Miss Heck while she persuaded me to come to the Training School." When the school moved to Lexington Road, the old sofa was placed in the recreation room. One cannot look at it now (if it has survived the recreation room!) without recalling with appreciation the part it played in a momentous decision for the new school.

With the important position of principal filled, the committee turned to other urgent matters. They met in Louisville in late July to approve the purchase of the building, map out the course of study, and select the special teachers. In addition to the courses at the Seminary, the following classes were to be taught at the Training School: personal work and vocal music by Mrs. McLure; piano and organ by Miss Julia McIver, from the faculty of Baylor College in Belton, Texas; elocution by Miss Louise Downer, of Louisville; domestic science by Miss Ellen Brown, of Louisville; and applied methods in city missions by Miss Emma Leachman, city missionary in Louisville.

While Mrs. Eager had taken the initiative in finding the principal, Mrs. Woody had the responsibility of supervising the repairs and getting the building in order for the opening. Since there was little money for furnishings, she appealed to the Baptist people of the city to give what they could spare. Many choice pieces of furniture came from some of the loveliest homes in the city. Other things, not so choice, were dragged out of attics. In true missionary spirit, everyone co-operated to get the building ready for the opening.

The Opening

The day before the guests and the students were to arrive Mrs. Woody and her three young sons worked far into the night to get the building ready for the opening. Among the guests for the occasion was the new corresponding secretary, Miss Edith C. Crane. A graduate of Bryn Mawr College, she had done student volunteer work before accepting the Woman's Missionary Union position. She was, therefore, deeply interested in mission work and particularly sympathetic with the purpose of the new school.

The honored guest was Miss Heck. She and Mrs. McLure were guests in the home of one of the Board members, sharing a room. Miss Heck had great hopes and plans for this school, and she talked far into the night about its development and the contribution it should make to missions at home and abroad. As Mrs. McLure listened and realized that she would be expected to lead in carrying out these ambitious plans, she turned her face to the wall and asked the Lord to let her die before morning! She could laugh over this experience in later years, but it was no laughing matter at the time.

The inaugural service was held on Wednesday evening, October 2, 1907, at the Broadway Baptist Church, two blocks from the Training School. In those days, and especially in Kentucky, church women did not speak or preside in mixed audiences, so Miss Heck asked Dr. Mullins to preside. It is interesting to sense in his opening remarks his conception of the school's special mission and its relationship to the Seminary. He congratulated the city, the South, and the world of Baptists upon the opening of such a school. He paid tribute to Dr. Simmons, to the Louisville women, and especially to the members of the first committee, Mrs. Woody, Mrs. Eager, Mrs. Whayne, Miss Broadus, Mrs. McGlothlin, Miss Fannie Moses, and Mrs. A. C. Cree. He called particular attention to the fact that "this institution is independent. . . . It is in no sense a branch of the Seminary." [2]

Other speakers on the program were Dr. B. D. Gray of the Home Mission Board, Dr. W. H. Smith of the Foreign Mission Board, and Dr. Carter Helm Jones, pastor of the Broadway Church. The climax of the program came in the presentation of a check from the Sunday School Board for $20,500 to cover the cost of the building. Dr. Frost, the secretary of the Board, had been a friend of the training school movement from the beginning and among its warmest champions during the years of bitter debate.

In his speech of presentation he revealed his faith in the far-reaching influence of the school as he said, ". . . This school is one of the mightiest agencies in God's world for the coming of His kingdom. . . . I rejoice to believe that God has used me and that is a blessed and humble thought."

Dr. Frost explained that the check from the Sunday School Board was given with the understanding that any balance in the Woman's Missionary Union building fund, after the repairs and necessary equipment had been paid for, should form the nucleus for an endowment fund.

The women had their special program the next morning in the Training School's chapel, which also served as social hall and classroom. Miss Heck presided and installed Mrs. McLure as principal of the school. The school's resident faculty members were introduced and reminded of the opportunities that were theirs in making their influence worldwide in their close association with the students. Talks were made by Mrs. Woody, who committed the school to Woman's Missionary Union; Mrs. McLure, and Miss Crane. Special prayers were offered for the school, Mrs. McLure, the faculty, staff members, and students by Mrs. Julian P. Thomas of Virginia, Mrs. J. D. Chapman of South Carolina, and Miss Broadus of Kentucky. The twenty students from ten states were presented by Miss Heck. They were asked to share their experience in dedicating their lives to missionary service.

These had been high hours, but the new principal and her co-workers and students must have heaved a united sigh of relief when the august visitors departed, leaving them free to get acquainted with each other and settle down to the work that had brought them together.

Important Foundations

As one looks at a great building, he rarely thinks of the effort that went into the foundations. Even so, as we review the history of Carver School of Missions, we are tempted to forget the planning that went into its foundations. As Mrs. McLure took up her unfamiliar duties, she found herself facing new and pressing problems daily, but she did not let the immediate difficulties dim the vision of the kind of school she had pictured as the ideal toward which she would reach. That ideal called for solid foundations on which the superstructure could be built through the years.

First of all, this was a school with a very special mission. Its purpose, as set forth in the first catalogue, was "to train women for efficient service in foreign, home and city missions and as church and Sunday School workers." Women who could work efficiently in this most important work must be given the best education possible. But the school had to make a beginning.

for the work in general, required a conscientious and realistic study of the student—her health record, emotional maturity, temperament, personality, and basic equipment. Mistakes have been made on both sides of the ledger, but at least the school has tried to encourage the best type of student to prepare for missionary service.

During its first year, the school was incorporated so that it could give certificates and diplomas and grant degrees to students who completed its prescribed courses of study. The curriculum committee had to create a new degree, since no degree had come into general use in missionary training schools. The Bachelor of Missionary Training degree was given for a two-year course of prescribed study, and the Master of Missionary Training for a three-year course. These degrees continued in use until the early thirties when the standard degrees in general religious education, Bachelor and Master of Religious Education, were adopted.

The curriculum of a growing school is never static. At the beginning the curriculum committee planned the course of study to meet the needs of the students as far as the resources permitted. Dr. Mullins and Dr. Carver advised as to the Seminary courses that should be included. Additional courses offered by the Training School were based on what similar schools were doing and what prospective workers needed to know. Mrs. McLure, with her practical approach to Christian work, tried to see that the school gave the students well-rounded preparation. The Seminary provided courses in Bible and related subjects, while the Training School added the more practical ones, such as music, elocution, personal work, and missionary education.

Mrs. McLure taught a class in sight-singing which was designed to help the girls learn to lead group singing as well as to select the best songs for various age groups. The hymns used in the chapel service introduced the students to a type of hymns to which many of them had not been exposed and developed in them an appreciation of the best in church music. Miss Julia McIver was employed to teach piano and organ (the old pump organ) with the hope that every girl would learn to play simple hymns.

The course in elocution, which later evolved into expression, and finally into public speaking, was designed to teach the girls how to be acceptable speakers. Mrs. McLure had no patience with a girl who stood before her audience and mumbled her words. While the classroom teacher tried to instil the principles of good speech, Mrs. McLure tried to see that these principles were carried out in practice. Students will remember that she always sat in the back of the chapel and that she did not hesitate to call, "Louder, please," if the leader was the soft-spoken variety. Once when one of these timid girls was reading, Mrs. McLure called, "Louder, please." Everybody laughed when the little voice piped out on her highest note, "Why do the heathen rage, and the people imagine a vain thing!"

The course in personal work started by Dr. Carver for the women at the Seminary a few years before was taken over by Mrs. McLure in 1907. Through the early years this course was unusually helpful to young women who had had little opportunity to study methods in this area of service.

The field work program was closely tied in with all the methods courses. Through this avenue the student learned to develop her skill in working with people. During the first year of the school each student was given three assignments each week in some mission or small church in the city. All students attended the report class, conducted by Mrs. McLure or Miss Leachman, and gave a report of her work. Problems were aired, and everyone learned from group experience.

Long before there was any definite course in missionary education, Mrs. McLure felt that the students should know the plan of organization and methods of work in Woman's Missionary Union. She would therefore drill the girls along these lines, using the leftover minutes when they were together in the chapel for other purposes.

In 1910, and for two years thereafter, Mrs. B. H. Dement, wife of one of the Seminary professors, was elected to teach mission study. In 1912 Mrs. Eager took over this responsibility and continued teaching for ten years. She gradually broadened the course by bringing Woman's Missionary Union workers to hold conferences on various parts of the work. In 1911 the president and the corresponding secretary of Woman's Missionary Union were asked to make annual visits to the school to talk to the students about the work of the Union. In this fashion the groundwork for the expanding curriculum was laid in the early years.

During the first years basic needs had to be met on a limited budget. It is not strange, therefore, that no request was made for an appropriation for starting a library until 1911.

Perhaps the mother of the scholarly Dr. Mullins was the first friend to remind the "powers that be" that no school could legitimately call itself an educational institution until it began to build a library. During the second session Mrs. Mullins sent a gift of $25.00 to be invested in reference books. The set of Bible commentaries bought with the gift is now well worn, a silent tribute to the lovely lady who provided help for innumerable chapel talks.

While progress was being made in the intellectual preparation of the students, Mrs. McLure was giving attention to other important phases of student growth. She was a deeply spiritual woman, free from fanatical ideas and wholesome in the expression of her faith. She believed in prayer and practiced it in her daily life. She desired above all things that the girls grow in spiritual power as they grew in knowledge of the Christian life.

The daily chapel service was as important as classes. Each student took her turn in leading the service. It was unthinkable that a student would deliberately stay away from chapel.

How could she be a leader in the world of the spirit if she did not put first things first in her own daily program? Habits of daily devotional life were encouraged. No sincere student could spend a year in the atmosphere of the school without becoming a better Christian as well as a better-trained worker.

In planning a well-rounded program for normal living and student development, Mrs. McLure did not forget the need for social life. From its beginning, a homelike atmosphere prevailed in the school. In those days hospitality was as natural a part of a home's routine as the three meals a day, and so it was in this home. There, denominational leaders and noted speakers coming to the city were entertained.

Students in those days stood greatly in awe of their teachers. Often, therefore, a professor and his wife were invited to the school for the evening meal. It was a wonderful experience, especially for the timid girls, to share the scintillating conversation at the table and see the great teacher in another light!

The hospitable homes of the professors were likewise often open to the girls by twos and threes for unforgettable dinner engagements. Again the timid girl might wonder if she would get choked at the table, or use the wrong piece of silver, or find her tongue paralyzed if she tried to enter into the conversation! The charming host and hostess were so natural that at once she was put at ease and she returned to tell her roommate what a perfectly lovely time she had at the home of "Dr. Bob" (the nickname of the great Greek scholar, Dr. A. T. Robertson).

The students were encouraged to plan their own social affairs, and they vied with each other in having unique parties. Mrs. Robertson, in writing about the school in 1912, said of its social life:

Any girl who has lived here a year must have learned . . . how to have a pretty "party" without extravagance. Twice in February the Training School gave a tea—on Valentine day to the married students and their wives, . . . and again during Miss Nancy Lee Swann's visit, when the leaders of the Y.W.A.'s of the city were asked to meet her. To serve afternoon tea charmingly is no small accomplishment, and to have everything delicious and up-to-date, yet inexpensive, is invaluable knowledge for any social or religious worker.[3]

The Training School party for the married students became an annual affair. The party for the young men in New York Hall was really the high occasion of the year. Student birthdays were observed in many clever ways in the dining room. School picnics were held in the beautiful city parks in the early fall or just before school closed. Surprise parties for new students usually marked Halloween. Mrs. McLure and the dietitian spared no effort to make Thanksgiving and Christmas dinners memorable occasions.

Many of the students of that era, especially the Seminary students, often complained of the rules which they thought too rigid. Mrs. Mullins tells an amusing story of four young "theologs" who called on Dr. Mullins one evening to enlist his help in changing the rules at the School. He listened "with a judicial air" until they finished, then he said:

Young gentlemen, I see clearly your point of view and your heartfelt desire to straighten out certain things at the Training School. You have come to me for help, but I am hampered by the fact that I have no authority over the management of this institution, and I am moved to wonder if any of you has been appointed arbiter of its regulations.[4]

In interpreting the rules of those early years restricting dating, one is tempted to forget the Victorian influence that colored the early years of this century. Mrs. McLure had lived in boarding schools, both as student and teacher, and she must have drawn on that experience in working out rules for the Training School.

If the rules were a bit more strict than contemporary schools, it should be remembered that she and the Board were still very close to the bitter controversy over locating the school in Louisville. If the contention of the opposition was that the relationship with the Seminary would tend to make it a match-making institution, then it must have been impressed upon her that she was responsible for seeing that this did not happen. It is easy to surmise the pressure that was brought to bear on her. Those who favored establishing the School in Louisville were most anxious to avoid any development that would give the opponents, few though they were, a chance to say, "I told you so!"

Some of the stories that have been enjoyed through the years have been at the expense of Seminary students who visited the school more or less regularly.

One such story is of a young man who lingered in the hall one wintry Sunday evening after the warning bell had rung. Finally, realizing that all the other boys had gone, he made a hasty exit. In his hurry he failed to button his overcoat and the heavy door closed on the corner of it. What should he do? The solemn nurse, Miss Coombs, was on duty that evening. He remembered the look she gave him as he hurried out and didn't have the nerve to ring the bell and face her again! He took out his knife, cut off the corner of his coat, and hurried down Broadway. The next day his roommate saw the overcoat and got the story.

Another young man came in one Sunday evening when Mrs. McLure was on duty. He hesitantly explained that he had made a date with one of the girls on Friday evening for church that evening, but he couldn't remember her name. Mrs. Mc-Lure got a list of the students and called the roll, but the poor chap shook his head—not a name rang a bell! Then Mrs. McLure facetiously asked him if he would like for her to call the girls down and line them up. Perhaps he would recognize the girl if he could see her! He balked at that and went to church alone. What about the girl? The story never gave her side of the affair!

Student government was initiated in the student body, probably during the third session, helping immeasurably in regulating the social life. The annual report in 1912 pointed out that under student government the year had been a most harmonious one.

The women of those days had to practice strict economy in their church work so, as a matter of course, they included only necessities in the Training School budget. For the first year Woman's Missionary Union appropriated $3,000 for the current expenses of the school. This amount continued to meet the needs until the 1913–1914 session when, due to the increased expenses to cover the operation of the Good Will Center, the Board asked for $3,600. In 1917–1918, when the School moved into the new and much larger building, the current expense appropriation was raised to $5,000.

In 1912 Mrs. Eager reported that the school had never had a deficit. In fact, it was a matter of pride on her part for the school always to live within its income. In order to do so, however, rigid economy had to be practiced. The School started with only two servants, a cook and a janitor, and this number was not increased until the School moved into the new building in 1917.

To live on this economical scale the students shared in the housework by serving the meals, washing dishes, setting tables, and sweeping and dusting the rooms of general use. In those early days the janitor tended the furnace and did the mopping and heavy cleaning. On Sunday he donned a white coat and served the dinner like a genteel butler.

For the most part, through the years the students have enjoyed the housework and have learned many valuable lessons in setting an attractive table and serving a well-planned meal. This sharing of work by all the students has promoted a democratic spirit in the school and has kept costs within the reach of all.

For the first two years Mrs. McLure was not only principal, teacher of personal work and sight-singing, hostess, housemother, and nurse, but office secretary as well. In the third year the Board provided for one of the students to help her in her routine correspondence. In the fall of 1913 Miss Heck noted the situation and recommended that the School secure a qualified secretary, who could also serve as treasurer.

It was an enforced economy to get along without a nurse. With the exception of two years the place was not filled satisfactorily until a practical nurse, Miss Ada Coombs, of Louisville, was secured in 1910. Many students during the following eighteen years have reason to remember with gratitude her quiet ministry.

Traditions

Traditions play an important part in the life of any school. Those held dear by students through the years began in the first decade. Perhaps the earliest was the "Chant," sung to the second graduating class in 1909 and to every class since then by their sister students. The "Chant" is an arrangement of Psalm 91 set to beautiful music. What graduate of the Training School, or Carver School, can ever forget the assurance in those eternal words?

> He shall give his angels charge over thee, to keep thee.
> Because thou hast made the Lord, Most High, thy habitation,
> There shall no evil befall thee.

The next in order was what came to be known as the Tuesday afternoon prayer meeting. In 1910, after the session was well started, Mrs. McLure felt that the atmosphere was less spiritual. Deeply concerned, she called the second-year students into her room one Tuesday afternoon and discussed the situation with them. Someone suggested that they meet every Tuesday afternoon, a half-hour before the evening meal, for special prayer. Gradually more and more of the students came in as they heard of the purpose of this informal prayer service. Year after year the group came together. Many former students, remembering the helpfulness of this prayer time, wrote back requesting prayer for themselves or problems in their work. So it came to be not only a time of prayer for the inner life of the school but also an opportunity to remember friends and co-workers around the world.

The beautiful custom of singing Christmas carols at the homes of the Seminary professors was begun in 1910. At that time carol singing was not as universally practiced as it is today, so it was a new and delightful experience to the students. In those days when students had little money for traveling, Christmas holidays were not given in the Seminary and Training School except for Christmas Eve and Christmas Day.

Carol singing on Christmas Eve was one way to prevent homesickness. The professors all lived within walking distance of the school. These singing visitors were a big surprise for the Seminary families the first year, but after that they began to look forward to this annual visit of Mrs. McLure and the girls.

For the students it was a never-to-be-forgotten experience to talk with Dr. Mullins in his library and examine the old rocker in which he did all his writing, to see Dr. Carver in the midst of his charming family, to eat old-fashioned peppermint stick candy at Dr. Sampey's, to see the famous New Testament scholar, Dr. Robertson, acting the part of a proud father and gracious host in his home. Mrs. Mullins vouched for the fact that this was the first Christmas carol singing in Louisville. The delightful custom continued until the school began to give Christmas holidays. After the Seminary moved to the Beeches, the students went by chartered bus to the scattered homes of the professors.

The processional, "Take the Light," was first sung at the 1912 commencement. This stirring processional is the final episode from the "Pageant of Darkness and Light," which was first presented at a great missionary conference in London. Similar conferences under the title "The World" were held in a few

American cities; the climax of each conference was the production of this pageant. In the spring of 1912 the "World in Cincinnati" brought this outstanding missionary production within easy traveling distance of Louisville.

Mrs. McLure wanted the girls to have this experience. She and Mrs. Eager studied the budget and discovered that they would close the year with a balance large enough to cover the expense of this trip for the entire school. What a lark it was to go and come on the river boat (cheap travel in those days), and what a memorable experience to see this moving pageant! Mrs. McLure, quick to grasp new ideas for her beloved school, used the processional at the commencement which came shortly after the trip to Cincinnati. It made a marvelous impression and has been used at every commencement since then. It is another reminder of the abiding missionary purpose of the School.

Mrs. McLure began spending her vacations at Chautauqua, New York, in the summer of 1909. It was there she found an inspiration for the "Vigil," the final dedication service for the graduates. The Readers' Guild at Chautauqua had developed an impressive recognition service for members completing a four-year course. They borrowed the idea for the service from the tales of the Knights of the Round Table. In symbolic fashion, Mrs. McLure took this idea and planned a meaningful consecration service for the graduates going out on their own great crusade. The first Vigil Service was held for the 1913 or 1914 class and has been repeated for every graduating class since that time.

Missionary Day and Praise Service have been a part of the life of the school from the very beginning. Missionary Day, a day set apart for special emphasis on missions, is a Seminary institution dating far back in its history. The Training School naturally joined with the Seminary in observing this day.

Stirred always by the addresses of missionaries, the students yearned for a service of their own in which they could give expression to their own spiritual needs and commitments. Seeking for a distinctive name for their services on the evenings of Missionary Days, they chose "Praise Service" as the best interpretation of what they wanted these worship experiences to be. The students elected their Praise Service leaders with as much concern as they chose their student government officers. The girls chosen took the assignment seriously and put their best into each service.

The Good Will Center

From the very beginning of her work in building the program of the Training School, Mrs. McLure put great emphasis on practical mission work in the city. She knew that training for service in the future required more than Bible study and its related subjects. Would-be missionaries must keep close to people, respond to the needs about them, and try to put into practice the lessons they were learning in the classroom. Among the many places where the students did their practical work was the Wesley House, the Methodist expression of the settlement house idea. Gradually Mrs. McLure began to think in terms of a Baptist settlement house operated by the School as a workshop for the students. It would give a freedom for experimentation that the missions in the city could not give, and it would open a new avenue of service in city missions.

After carefully considering the idea, she presented the subject to the local Board of Managers. It appealed to them and they, in turn, discussed it with the General Board of the School at its annual meeting in Oklahoma City in May, 1912. As a result, the following recommendation was adopted by the Union when the Training School report was given: "That the Board be authorized to establish an Industrial School in which our students can get practical training for themselves while they are giving helpful service."

In preparation for starting this work, the first of its kind among Southern Baptists, Mrs. McLure studied in the New

York School of Philanthropy during the summer of 1912. In order to see a social settlement in operation, she boarded in a settlement on the East Side. Informed on the current theories in social betterment and enthusiastic over the possibilities in the settlement house plan, she returned to Louisville to start the new work at the Center with the plus of the Christian faith.

During the summer a committee of the Board located and rented a small house at 512 East Madison Street, within easy walking distance of the school. It was thoroughly cleaned and renovated and made an attractive center for the work. The name chosen at first, the Baptist Training School Settlement, was placed conspicuously over the door. The neighborhood had watched the work with curious interest. The people in the immediate section were personally invited by Training School students in a program of visitation.

On the opening night, October 25, the small assembly room was crowded. The street boys particularly were there, and they were getting so noisy that the poor girl in charge of the program turned to Mrs. McLure in desperation. Fortunately, it was a warm evening and she had brought her folding fan along. She rose quickly and, pointing at the boys with her fan, said in a stern voice, "You boys must keep quiet or you will have to leave."

Immediately the boys quieted down and the program proceeded. According to her humorous account of the incident, she then went into a back room where a group of students were waiting, and said with much complacency, "See, you have got to be firm with these street boys!"

A bit later she went back into the assembly room, this time with the fan open. One of the boys said, "Huh, I thought she had a butcher knife in her hand!"

Miss Leachman, the city missionary, established her office in the settlement house and gave invaluable aid to Mrs. McLure in directing the girls in their many activities with the children and young people. She led the Mother's Club, which for years was the strongest and most influential group in the work.

Within a year the work outgrew the rented quarters and a house was bought at 524 East Madison for $5,000. Funds for the purchase were taken from the small endowment fund, and the rent formerly paid reimbursed the fund at 6 per cent interest. This two-story house, with a few changes, served the work adequately for several years.

Mrs. H. M. Wharton, chairman of the Personal Service Committee of Woman's Missionary Union, recommended in 1914 that the settlements conducted by Woman's Missionary Union workers be known as "Good Will Centers." Consequently, the mother settlement at the Training School began its work that fall under the new name.

God's Best Gift

The investment of friendship in an institution endures long after the gift of money has been forgotten. The year 1912 was a year to be remembered because it brought such an investment in the person of Miss Kathleen Mallory. Miss Crane had resigned as corresponding secretary of Woman's Missionary Union, and Miss Mallory, secretary of the Alabama Union, was elected to fill the position. For thirty-six years she served the School as a member of its Board of Trustees with loyalty and devotion. Through two building campaigns she marshaled the financial resources of the Union. To three principals she was a friend and counselor, and to hundreds of students she was the finest example of dedication to the cause of missions.

In 1914 a new member who was to serve the School as matron, dietitian, and house director for a total of nineteen years came to the staff. Miss Mary Mitchell took over her new job shortly before the session opened, and everything in her department was working smoothly by the time the students arrived. The girls were grateful for her quiet efficiency and kind supervision. Miss Mitchell's co-workers through the years were thankful for her devotion to duty, her ability and willingness to make the best of difficult situations, and her practice of economy when it was a virtue to be praised.

Enlargement

As one reads the story of the School, enlargement seems to be its theme song. The emphasis was never on building up the enrolment for the sake of numbers. The aim was rather to find students qualified physically, intellectually, and spiritually to become the sort of workers needed in many fields of service.

The building, bought in 1907, could house comfortably forty students and four staff members. During the second session forty students were enrolled and, evidently, the correspondence with applicants indicated a larger student body for the next year. Woman's Missionary Union met in Louisville in 1909, giving many women their first opportunity to see the School. The Board of Trustees met with the local Board of Managers in the Training School chapel. From that meeting came the first urgent call for enlargement during the summer of 1910. The sum of $35,000 was designated as needed for the building fund, and this total was apportioned among the states. Plans were made for presenting needs to the societies, and the hope was expressed that enlargement could begin in the summer of 1910.

At this stage their plans did not go beyond necessary additions to the building to house the slowly growing student body. The General Board, at its meeting in Baltimore in 1910, left the details of such planning with the local Board. They were instructed to finance any additions and repairs out of the first receipts of the enlargement fund. As a matter of fact, the program had already started in the building of a new kitchen.

By the time the Board met in annual session in Jacksonville, Florida, in 1911, building plans were thrown into confusion by developments at the Seminary. During the year the Seminary had purchased property outside the city on Brownsboro Road. Some felt that the School should stay close to the

Seminary; therefore, property should be bought adjacent to the Seminary site. Others felt that to move so far out of the city would cut the students off from any opportunity for doing practical mission work.

The debate was finally settled by the appointment of a special committee, with power to act, composed of the president and secretary of the Union; Miss Evie Brown, of Tennessee; Mrs. B. F. Proctor, of Kentucky; and Mrs. Eager, Mrs. Woody, and Mrs. Marvin, of the local Board. This committee was instructed to consult the Advisory Board, then to purchase either property adjacent to the Seminary's new site or the corner building next to the School building on Broadway.

For the next two years nothing was said about immediate enlargement. The decision not to buy the property on Brownsboro Road proved to be eminently wise. The Seminary, after more sober reflection, decided that the location was too far out of town for convenience and so gave up any idea of moving for the time being.

The high hour in plans for enlargement came at the annual session of Woman's Missionary Union in Nashville in 1914. Women were cautious in those days. The local Board wanted to be sure that they had a solid reason for asking for so much for their beloved School. The enrolment in the fall of 1913 gave them their best argument. As applications continued to come in during the summer, it became evident that extra rooms would have to be secured. Fortunately, quarters could be rented directly across the street, and when the session opened, twenty girls found themselves assigned to these rented rooms. Everything was too crowded in the main building for comfort and good work, however, so plans began to take shape for launching the building campaign.

In April Miss Heck went to Louisville to consider with the local Board this all-important question. She was enthusiastic and, with Mrs. McLure, worked out the program for the presentation of the School at the annual meeting. A part of the plan provided for the student body to go to Nashville. It is not a matter of record that traveling expenses were provided but, in all probability, they were, since the average student then got along on the proverbial shoestring. But the students got there somehow, and the hospitable women of Nashville entertained them as if they were already missionaries.

The School was given a choice morning hour on the Woman's Missionary Union program held in McKendree Methodist Church. The students who were not helping on the program were seated in the balcony. A playlet, "The Beginning of a New Session," an episode in two scenes, was presented by some of the students. Then the balcony group sang a favorite Training School hymn, "God Is Working His Purpose Out," and the lovely commencement Chant.

This drama and pageantry provided the background for Mrs. Eager to give her report and make the appeal for the new building. She explained that the corner lot and building had been bought for $20,142. The plans were conservative. One wing of a future building on this corner lot could be built for $75,000, which would include necessary alterations on the old building and a new heating plant adequate for both buildings. This plan would provide for a hundred students.

The report stimulated much discussion, all of it friendly. Those were the days of pledges from the floor. The first pledge was made by the alumnae for $500. Then, after a whispered conference among some of the students, Mary Northington rose from her balcony seat, stepped quickly to the railing, and pledged $1,000 from the student body. Mrs. McLure said later that she nearly fainted! Those foolish girls! Where did they think they would get so much money? But get it they did, by begging and by giving liberally out of their meager resources.

The local Board had really started the fund-raising before the annual meeting with their pledge of $1,000. Mrs. McLure added $100, which represented more than a month's salary. Mrs. H. H. Tift, of Georgia, a lifelong friend of the School, pledged $1,000; Mrs. T. T. Hyde, of South Carolina, $500. What a spine-tingling hour it was! Before the meeting closed, over two-thirds of the needed amount was pledged.

Among the contributions for enlargement was a gift of $10,-000 from the Sunday School Board, an evidence of the continued interest of its beloved secretary, Dr. Frost.

Miss Heck's career as the president of Woman's Missionary Union reached its climax at the Nashville meeting where she gave the Training School the place of honor on her program. Before the 1915 meeting she was critically ill and passed away in August of that year. The School lost a great friend not only for the immediate building plans but for the long future. From its adoption in 1907 she continued to have an enlarging vision of its development and usefulness. One wonders if its future would have been materially different if she could have continued to have a voice in its affairs through another decade.

The decision of the Union to make the chapel of the new building a memorial to her drastically changed the plans for the proposed building. Such a memorial must be at the very center of the building. The building committee, therefore, at the 1916 meeting in Asheville, North Carolina, recommended that the two buildings at 334 East Broadway be razed and the building that had been planned for future completion be erected at once, at an approximate cost of $150,000.

Plans had been worked out to raise the needed cash by organizing "dollar clubs" with the slogan, "$98,000 from 98,000 Baptists." A playlet, "Lifting the Sky Line," written and directed by one of the students, Willie Jean Stewart, was presented by a group of students. Tailored for the occasion, it suggested practical ways of raising the $98,000.

The amazing innovation, however, was the plan to carry the campaign to the floor of the Southern Baptist Convention. A half-hour of the time of the evening program for home missions was allotted to the Training School. Whether the women asked for the time or Dr. Gray offered it is not known, but he was a friend of the School and was gracious in taking it under the wing of home missions in this questionable method of enlisting the help of the men.

Dr. Lansing Burrows, president, presided and called on Dr. Boyce Taylor of Kentucky (who, as everyone knew, violently opposed women's speaking in religious assemblies) to lead in prayer. Did he do it with malice aforethought? He was known as a man with a keen sense of humor! He then presented Miss Kathleen Mallory, who in turn introduced Mrs. McLure. The lights were turned out and pictures depicting Training School history, life, and work and its former students in their far-flung fields of service were thrown on the screen. Mrs. Mc-Lure stepped up on a box and explained the pictures in a clear voice, though she confessed later that her knees were trembling so that she feared any minute she would fold up and fall off.

Dr. Mullins then took the floor and presented the building plans and program, explaining that the women needed $98,-000 for their new building and proposed to get it from 98,000 men! He added that Dr. Gambrell claimed the privilege of giving the first dollar. An offering was taken, and four hundred dollar bills started the "dollar clubs" boom.

In this fashion it came about that Miss Mallory and Mrs. McLure, in the interest of the Training School, had the honor of being the first women ever to speak to the Southern Baptist Convention, though some of the brethren considered it a doubtful honor. In fact, the ultraconservative minority described the incident as "glorying in their shame."

Immediately the Baptist papers reflected the reaction of the people in various sections. The *Baptist Courier* did not become excited but reported the famous session in a calm manner. The writer got the message, and that was the important thing. He said of the pictures,

I cannot give much of an idea of these pictures. They were not of a very high order from the standpoint of art but they accom-

plished their purpose . . . We saw the prospective new building
. . . and all the buildings the school had used . . . We were carried into class rooms, saw groups of girls, visited their houses for
good will work, followed the graduates to their far-off fields of
labor and saw them with their classes, in their kindergartens and
mingling in all the life they had gone to redeem.[5]

J. B. Moody said in *The Baptist Advance:*

It was expected that some would scowl and growl and howl . . .
Women are entitled to "knowledge" and to "approve" and disap-
prove, and to an expression of it. . . . The prohibition of women
"speaking before mixed assemblies" comes out of a heretical notion
inherited from those who were lacking in knowledge and sound
judgment on this subject.[6]

Perhaps the finest defense came from Dr. Gambrell in the
Baptist Standard, the organ of Baptists of Texas. His article,
"Women Speaking in Mixed Assemblies," said in part:

One of the thrills of the Asheville Convention was brought on by
two of our very finest women, who spoke to the Convention about
a work important to the kingdom . . . This so displeased some of
the brethren, that, if some of the editors are correct, many voted
against the report of woman's work later, as a rebuke to the women,
who, in the thinking of the rebukers, had done an unscriptural and
shameful thing . . .
    Let's quit nagging the sisters on an impossible interpretation
and encourage them to walk in the liberty of the Spirit with us.[7]

All this seems foolish and amusing with the gulf of time sep-
arating this day from that, but it was a serious matter to the
minority who believed that they were called upon to "defend
the faith." In the end, the controversy played into the hands
of the women and gained many contributions for the needed
building.

The School was fortunate in the election of Mrs. W. C.
James as president of the Union in 1916. Her wise planning and

sound judgment were valuable assets to the School during the building campaign. She was a Texan by birth, but she had lived since 1907 in Virginia, where her husband was pastor of one of Richmond's large churches. She had been president of the Virginia Woman's Missionary Union for two years. She came into her office as president when wise leadership was needed, and she measured up to its demands in a remarkable way.

It was no easy matter to plan for the 1916–1917 session. Fortunately, three houses were found in the same block across the street, and in August the equipment and furnishings were moved out of the two buildings that were soon to be demolished and into the three houses. There must have been many headaches involved in planning a temporary home under such conditions, but efficient Miss Mitchell was equal to the task. Mrs. McLure returned early from vacation to help work out the best arrangements, and well in advance of the opening the houses were ready and livable.

Letters were sent to all applicants, warning them that unless they were willing and able "to endure hardness as a good soldier of the cross," not to come. The rooms would be crowded, there would be few conveniences, food would be plain because of limited facilities for cooking. In spite of this warning, sixty students entered and proved by their fine adjustment and ready acceptance of the inconveniences that they were "good soldiers."

In addition to the normal difficulties of operating a school under such conditions, World War I had been in progress for two years and the position of the United States was becoming more untenable. Food was scarce and expensive. The gas pressure was poor. Miss Mitchell got up early and did the major baking for the day before the cook arrived and before other houses in the block began to use the gas. Because of this type of service and sacrifice, at Thanksgiving the student body, under the leadership of their chairman, Mary Alexander, of

Texas (who later became one of the most valuable missionaries to China) voted to express their appreciation of the "self-denial and struggle of our faculty and Board in providing even the everyday necessities for us."

No finer class has ever been graduated from the Training School than that of 1917. Eight of the twenty-two members became foreign missionaries, and one has been described by her state trustee as one of the most effective and Christlike home missionaries she has ever known. Others of that illustrious group have done outstanding work in many types of Christian service.

In spite of mounting costs of material, the decision to build had been made, and the work went forward according to the plans. On November 5, 1916, excavating started, and through the long, hard winter the building began to take shape. On April 5, just three days after the United States entered the war, the ceremony for laying the cornerstone was held in the Broadway Christian Church in the same block. In spite of the bitter cold wind and rain, many people attended the service, including representatives of the three boards. Mrs. Woody, the chairman of the Building Committee, laid the first trowel of mortar after the box with its precious documents had been placed in the cornerstone. Over the stone was the inscription, "That our daughters may be as cornerstones, hewn after the fashion of a palace."

The program in the church included talks by Dr. Mullins and Dr. Van Ness, who presented for the Sunday School Board a check for $10,000, its third gift to the School. During the winter Louisville Baptists had put on a great campaign in which more than $30,000 was given to the building fund.

The student body of sixty members made amazing contributions out of their limited resources. In addition to their gift of $250 to the Louisville campaign, they sent $640 to the treasurer of Woman's Missionary Union. In three years of the building campaign the students contributed a total of $2,168.65. By agreement this gift was added to that of the alumnae to build and furnish the apartment for the principal.

It was the middle of September before the new building could be occupied. There were no lights, no locks, and in some cases, no doors, but Mrs. McLure and Miss Mitchell lived by candlelight for a few days and trusted the night watchman for protection. In two weeks the students would be arriving. The old furnishings had to be moved from the three houses across the street, the necessary new furniture and equipment bought, and the new building put in order.

Since the entire building was not needed, the west wing was rented to the Young Women's Christian Association to be used as a residence for women who came to the city to see the young men who were in training in Camp Taylor.

By spring the building was finally completed. Open house was held on March 12, when more than four hundred local people came to see and went away to praise. Many felt like the little boy from the Good Will Center who, with his group, came to see the building at the invitation of his teacher. As they entered the lobby and looked toward the marble stairway bathed in golden light from the beautiful stained glass window behind it, he said in awed tones, "Say, fellers, ain't this a palace?"

The dedication was planned for May 22 so that people attending the Convention and the annual session of Woman's Missionary Union in Hot Springs could return to their homes by way of Louisville, and they came in large numbers. The program was long because the eyes of the denomination had been focused on the School during the building campaign and almost everyone had put something into its building. Dr. T. B. Ray and Dr. B. D. Gray spoke of the relationship of the School to the Foreign and Home boards. Dr. Van Ness of the Sunday School Board presented the portrait of Dr. Frost, to whom the Training School was an abiding interest and conviction. Miss Broadus had the honor of accepting the portrait for the school.

Dr. Mullins, of course, was on the program. His service as a staunch friend was universally recognized and appreciated. Mrs. J. D. Boushall, of Raleigh, a sister of Miss Heck, presented her portrait for the beautiful Heck Memorial Chapel, and Mrs. W. C. James responded. Brief greetings were brought by Mrs. W. N. Jones, of North Carolina; Mrs. J. G. Jackson, of Arkansas; Mrs. H. H. Tift, of Georgia; and two former students, Miss Mary Northington and Miss Willie Jean Stewart. The main address of the morning was brought by Miss Kathleen Mallory.

At the evening service a pageant, written by Miss Margaret Lackey, of Mississippi, was presented by the students under Mrs. McLure's direction. It gave the history of the School in fourteen scenes, beginning with the dream of Dr. Simmons and ending with this great day of dedication.

In the early days when the School was housed in the old building bought for its first home, someone (Miss Heck, according to tradition) called it the "House Beautiful." Originally this title described the spirit of the place rather than its physical appearance. With the beautiful Gothic building completed, the name "House Beautiful" came into universal use. Perhaps no building in Southern Baptist life has been so beloved. Every Woman's Missionary Union member gave something to it during the campaign for funds and, consequently, had a personal interest in it. The following story may well illustrate how the average woman felt about it.

Many years after the building was completed there appeared at the door one summer day a little lady from the deep South, asking if this was House Beautiful. On being assured by the secretary that it was, she said, "My husband and I were driving through and I told him I wanted to see House Beautiful. He said we did not have time to stop, but I told him I would cry if he did not give me time to see it. He is waiting across the street and I must hurry. Will you show me around?"

Miss Ruth Maness, the secretary, graciously invited her in and started on a tour. She tried to tell the little lady what she was seeing, but the visitor kept talking so fast that finally Miss Maness gave up. When they got back to the front door the little lady, all a-flutter, said, "Now, honey, will you tell me in a few words what I have seen, so I will know what to tell the missionary society at our next meeting?"

The first commencement was held in the Heck Memorial Chapel on June 3, 1918, with Mrs. W. C. James as the speaker and Mrs. McLure for the first time presenting the diplomas. This was indeed a new era! Heretofore commencements had been held in beautiful old Broadway Baptist Church, with a Seminary professor delivering the address and another giving the diplomas. Now in their own chapel, the women were free to plan their own programs.

An old era was ending, a new one was beginning. It had indeed been a decade of growth in many ways since May, 1907, when Woman's Missionary Union launched its great "venture of faith." A total of $183,536.76 had been invested in this beautiful building that their daughters might be "hewn after the fashion of a palace."

3

The Test of Change

In this world of change naught which comes stays, and naught which goes is lost.—Madame Swetchine

In the spring of 1918, when the beautiful new building was dedicated, the future looked promising for the School. In spite of war, a dream had been realized; a goal had been attained. Woman's Missionary Union was united in its enthusiastic support of its beloved project. The successful conclusion of the building campaign had demonstrated that the School had the good will of the entire denomination.

Mrs. McLure was there, mature in her direction of the work, with a resident staff thoroughly versed in their duties. The summer correspondence indicated that a record enrolment would mark the opening of the twelfth session. To all appearances the School was now ready to fulfil its original purpose, that of preparing women missionaries in adequate numbers to meet the calls of the boards.

The shadows of sinister war clouds, however, had already cast a pall of sorrow over the School and set in motion a series of events that would bring drastic changes. Just as the session closed shortly after the dedication, Mrs. McLure received news that her only son had been seriously wounded in France. All summer long he was undergoing surgery for facial wounds and a badly shattered leg.

On the opening day of the fall session Mrs. Woody received the news that her son, Wallace, had been killed in France.

78

Young, handsome, and having just started in a successful newspaper career, he was typical of the youth of the world who were sacrificed to the god of war. It seemed such a short time since Wallace and his brothers, McIver and Albert, mere boys, had worked so valiantly with their mother to make the first building ready for the opening in October, 1907.

War Work

Mrs. McLure, like all mothers of that period, was deeply patriotic. She placed her service star in her window with sacrificial pride. When the Young Men's Christian Association asked her in late September to take over the training and supervision of the women who would be working in the camps in the southeastern region, she took counsel with her heart and felt that it was God's call to the service of her country.

In conference with Mrs. Eager and Mrs. Woody, plans were worked out to present to the local Board for approval at its October meeting. Mrs. Eager was to be in charge, spending a part of every day at the School. Mrs. G. W. Perryman, a widow of a Baptist minister in Kentucky, was to live in the School as the housemother. Miss Leachman, who had from the beginning assisted with the field work of the students, would have entire charge of this part of the work.

Miss Mallory went to Louisville for the Board meeting and shared with the local women the responsibility of granting Mrs. McLure the year's leave of absence and approving the plans for the year. Mrs. McLure's salary was to be divided between Mrs. Eager and Mrs. Perryman.

The shock and sorrow of the Board was mild compared to that of the students when, shortly after the Board meeting, they were called to the chapel to hear the amazing plans. Shock left them speechless, but tears left no doubt as to how they felt. At a called meeting later that evening the students voted to express in a letter what they could not say face to face.

Mrs. McLure was so much a part of the total life of the School that it was natural that Board and students alike wondered how they could carry on without her. She had started with a mere twenty students and no staff to help with the details of organized school work, so in the first years she had to direct everything. She continued with this many-sided job until the growth of the student body justified the addition of staff members to share the work with her.

One young girl expressed in blunt words what many may have thought. Soon after arrival, she found Mrs. McLure in the little office and inquired where she was to register.

Mrs. McLure said, "I'll take care of that."

When that was done the student asked who would tell her about her field work.

"I'll take care of that," was the answer.

Then the girl wanted to know about paying her board.

"I'll take care of that, too," said the unruffled principal.

The unsophisticated girl looked at the dignified lady and, without a trace of embarrassment, said, "You must be the whole cheese!"

These girls of 1918 pulled themselves together and planned a fitting farewell service for their beloved principal. In keeping with the times, the service must not be gay, but neither must it be sad. Since pageantry had become the popular way of putting on a program, they solved their dilemma by hastily planning a program of music, song, and story under the title, "The Lady of the Happy Heart." Pearl Todd wrote the words, Rose Goodwin set them to music, and Effie Chastain directed the production.

The pageant depicted the procession of former students who had taken the good news into many parts of the world until war intervened. Liberty came on the scene calling for help, and the spirits of Faith, Hope, and Love went down in the audience, found Mrs. McLure, put a regal robe around her shoulders, a lighted candle in her hand, and escorted her to the platform, where she was given the charge, "Go with Liberty and with your light guide her to the nations of the world."

With the ready response that was so characteristic of her, she stepped into the part and spoke as if the words were in the script: "May I, as your representative, hold my light so low that none may miss the way and so high that Jesus Christ may see and glorify it as his radiant light to the world."

There was but one conclusion to so meaningful a service. The students took up the familiar and compelling strains of the processional, "Take the Light." As the singers reached the climax in the stirring high notes of the "wonder and the glory of the light," there was a pause, and then from behind a screen came softly the strains of the beloved chant, "He Shall Give His Angels Charge over Thee." As Mrs. McLure had sent her students out into service each year, they were now sending her with the same high charge and promise of God's blessing.

And so they sent her out to help win the war, and someone facetiously remarked that it was won in two weeks! Indeed, the Armistice was signed a mere two weeks later. Since the women would continue in Young Men's Christian Association work for several months, Mrs. McLure stayed with her assignment through the year. The class of 1919 had the joy of having her come back to deliver the commencement address.

New Relationship to the Seminary

With the war over the demand for trained workers was becoming insistent. Mission fields were calling for workers again, and new avenues of service were opening in the home field. All of the 1919 graduates were employed in their chosen fields before the end of the session. As a consequence, the enrolment jumped from eighty-two boarding students and twenty-four day students in 1918 to one hundred and twenty-seven boarding and thirty-seven day students in 1919.

This unexpected success posed a grave problem for the Seminary and the Training School. The Seminary's attendance was growing in the same proportion, and the two large student groups were taxing the classrooms. Moreover, the dormitory in the new House Beautiful would care for only 117 girls comfortably. Here they were in the third year in the new building, and ten girls had to be crowded in where no space had been provided for them. Had the women of that day been motivated by too little faith and too much caution? We should remember that they built during a world war. How could anyone foresee when it would end and what conditions would grow out of it?

The immediate Seminary problem was as unexpected and difficult to solve. The small faculty was being overburdened with work. In conference with Dr. Mullins, a plan was worked out whereby Woman's Missionary Union would pay to the Seminary the next year $4,000 to help with the salary of two assistant professors and provide for additional help in grading papers.

The future problem was more difficult to work out. Ten years before, the Seminary had bought property outside the city. It had to be decided at that time whether the School would move so that an available site near that of the Seminary could be secured. As advantages and disadvantages were weighed, the decision was made to stay in the city where the students would be close to field work appointments.

The School was small at the time; the Seminary's move was in the distant future. When that problem finally had to be faced, the Board felt sure it would be possible to send forty or fifty students by streetcar to Seminary classes. Feeling secure in their decision, the Union, on the recommendation of the General Board of the School, projected the building campaign in 1914 on the downtown location.

Now that the war was over, plans began to develop for a building campaign for the Seminary. Training School enrolment had already gone far beyond expectations. No streetcar service was provided to the Seminary property, and "other obstacles," which Mrs. Eager did not name in her annual report, appeared on the horizon to upset the peace of mind of the management.

So the committee appointed to iron out the immediate problem of crowded conditions with the Seminary also took up the future problem with Dr. Mullins. He was sympathetic and helpful, as always. Out of that discussion a tentative plan was suggested whereby the senior professors would give lectures and junior professors would conduct regular classes in the Training School classrooms, if the Union would "provide sufficient assistance" for such an arrangement. The Seminary was flexible and ready to go the second mile.

Staff Changes

An immediate problem at the close of the 1919–1920 session was the resignation of Miss Mary Mitchell as dietitian and housekeeper. She had been with the School since 1914 and had given stability to the home life following a series of changes in that department. She loved the School and had turned down "flattering offers," said Mrs. Eager in her annual report, but one had now come which was "too tempting to resist."

Mrs. Eager prided herself on finding suitable people for places of service and leadership, and the facts usually proved that she was right in her judgment and appraisal. In this case, her thoughts were directed to Miss Mary Louise Warren, who had been brought up on a large farm in the bluegrass section of Kentucky. After her father's death, Miss Warren continued to operate the farm. Mrs. Eager had seen her preside with dignity and charm in her own home. At the time the School opened in 1907 she was present as the state Sunbeam leader.

Mrs. Eager's leadership was typical of her driving personality. When she went after a person, that person might as well give in sooner, for she would have to do so later. Miss Warren had never thought of being an employed person, but well in advance of the opening of the session in 1920, she was established in the School and learning by hard experience how to manage a large institution. Mrs. Eager's choice was eminently justified during the sixteen years that Miss Warren served the School as dietitian and house director.

About the same time, Mrs. George W. Sutterlin came to the faculty as a part-time teacher of expression. She tried valiantly to improve the diction of the girls. One day in class she made an effort to teach a pretty Georgia brunette how to say "girl." A few days later when the students were doing stunts, the little Georgian evened the score with Mrs. Sutterlin by saying, "I've learned one thing in expression. I'll never say 'gull' again. After this I'll say woman!"

Miss Leachman Leaves Louisville

In midsummer of 1921 Miss Leachman made a decision that changed the whole current of her life and drastically affected the life of the School. She had been asked by Dr. Gray at the Southern Baptist Convention in May to come to the Home Mission Board as its first general field worker. She returned to Louisville to think it over.

She weighed the opportunities and sought the will of the Lord. She had been city missionary under the Kentucky State Mission Board since 1904. She had gone to live in the little training school home that year in order to have the companionship of like-minded friends. When Woman's Missionary Union adopted the School in 1907, she was asked to continue to live in the School as the teacher of applied methods in city missions. In 1909 she was voted an honorarium of $100 a year in addition to her room and board.

All through these years she had assisted Mrs. McLure with the field work appointments and supervision. When the Good Will Center was opened in 1912, she set up her office as city missionary in that building. She took over more responsibility for the Center as the growing School claimed more of Mrs. McLure's attention.

Now as she thought over her life and work, she felt that she had "got in a rut," as she expressed it, and the new work with the Home Mission Board offered a challenging opportunity. So she severed her connection with the Kentucky State Mission Board, which was her major work, sent her resignation to Mrs. Eager, talked her plans over with Mrs. McLure, and before the majority of people knew what was happening she had moved to Atlanta.

Miss Leachman was a dynamic personality, and she made a unique contribution to the School, especially to the students who had come and gone during these seventeen years. The girls either loved her or they were deathly afraid of her. Her criticism could be as biting as her praise was genuine.

She had worked hard to prepare herself for what she wanted to do, but what she lacked in formal education she made up in self-education. As city missionary she spent her time on street-cars and at transfer points reading. She had no patience with a worker who would not keep up with world affairs by reading current books and magazines. Of one former student, who had gone into Woman's Missionary Union work, she said, "It is evident that she has not read anything but the Standard of Excellence since she took that job!"

This vital, devoted personality would be sadly missed in Louisville. For many years the loves of her life had been the Training School and Woman's Missionary Union. Now she added the Home Mission Board and gave to it devoted and constructive service until 1940 when a heart condition forced her to retire.

She spent the last years of her life at a nursing home in Louisville. She suffered greatly, but pain did not lessen her love for her Lord and the causes that had been so dear to her through the years. She was a great believer in prayer and could talk amazingly intimately to the Lord and about him. One day when a friend went to see her, she found her just recovering from a bad attack. In typical fashion she said, "I thought I was going to die this morning, but I told the Lord not to take me today. I wasn't ready to meet him, for I had been in a bad humor all morning." In August, 1952, death brought to an end a life that had been rich in service and rewarding in friendships.

For several years before Miss Leachman left the school there had been a growing need for a full-time director in the practical missions department, which would include the Good Will Center. The spare time that Mrs. McLure and Miss Leachman together could give to it was totally inadequate as the enrolment increased. Now that the School was face to face with the problem of finding that person, it was no easy matter. Naturally, they would at that stage want a graduate of the School who would be thoroughly versed in its purposes and ideals, but few alumnae had had experience in this field.

As they searched their memories and their files, attention was called to a young woman in South Carolina who had been a member of the 1915 class. She had done settlement work in textile communities in Georgia for five years. Hardly realizing what was happening to her, Carrie U. Littlejohn found herself back in Louisville in September, 1921. She assisted the principal by taking over the personal evangelism and social work classes, as well as the supervision of the practical work and the direction of the Good Will Center.

Enlargement Again

Following the war the enrolment increased until the peak was reached during the 1921–1922 session with one hundred and forty-two boarding students and forty-four day students. To take care of the overflow, the house next door was bought for $18,000. Even with this extra house, students were crowded into every available space. A classroom became a bedroom for four; a third girl was put into each of the larger rooms; the first floor and attic next door became the Annex.

The larger enrolment again brought to the forefront plans for enlargement. In 1920 a thorough study was made of the building by a special committee composed of Mrs. James, Miss Mallory, Mrs. Lowndes, two men from the Advisory Committee, and representatives from the Seminary faculty. Captain Brinton B. Davis, the architect, presented plans for extending the west wing back to the alley, a four-story addition that would provide for another hundred students. Because of the prohibitive prices of labor and material, however, he advised that this building program be postponed. Later events proved that it was providential that the School did not proceed with these enlargement plans, for the enrolment began to taper off at once. After 1923 the enlargement of the downtown building was not mentioned again.

Provision was made for Dr. and Mrs. Eager to live in the second floor apartment of the house next door, bought in 1921. Mrs. T. G. Bush, the Alabama trustee, presented the matter to Woman's Missionary Union in the following resolution:

That in recognition of the years of loving and unparalleled service of Mrs. Eager as Chairman of the local Board of Managers, Financial Secretary and Member of Faculty, an apartment in the adjoining house with board be offered to Dr. and Mrs. Eager. Their presence among the students would mean daily blessing and benediction to the school.[1]

Mrs. McLure's Resignation

The many changes that had come to the School during this period faded into insignificance in comparison with the shattering prospect of losing Mrs. McLure. The members of the local Board, especially Mrs. Eager and Mrs. Woody, had worked in such close association with her that they could not imagine the School without her. Through the multitude of problems of the early and growing years, the difficult building campaign, and the postwar period, she was there, meeting them with poise and optimism and the strength that grows out of a deep religious faith.

For the alumnae, Mrs. McLure *was* the School. Many of

them were very close to her during student days and loved her devotedly. Some of them stood in awe of her and never paid her a visit unless called in for conference. But without question, they all admired her and had the utmost confidence in her administration of affairs.

Several factors entered into Mrs. McLure's decision to retire. Perhaps the most decisive was the changing conditions of the postwar period. The School could not expect to escape the drastic changes that the war brought to the old way of life. There were new attitudes toward authority, new ideas of freedom, new and aggressive desires for self-expression. Students were not revolutionary in their efforts to introduce a new pattern of life in the School, but there was constant pressure from within, an evident restlessness, creating an atmosphere with which she found it difficult to cope. This was a new experience to her, and a disturbing one.

Transitions are never easy for those most vitally affected. This one was not easy for the students, products of their day and generation. It was difficult for Mrs. McLure. She belonged to the old school, and she could not accept happily the changes that the new day was bringing. The conviction slowly came to her that it was time for a younger woman to take over.

One of the compelling reasons for her decision was a personal one. Her only son, Tom, had been in hospitals in France and the United States for three years, having his face and right leg repaired after being wounded in the spring of 1918. This long, emotion-packed period had drained her of strength needed sorely for guiding the School through the transition years.

In 1921 Captain McLure was finally dismissed from the hospital, and he secured a position with the Kentucky Highway Commission as a civil engineer, the profession for which he had been prepared in college. Under the circumstances, the conviction grew on Mrs. McLure that she should make a home for him in this nomadic life that he would be living, and he entered into her plans with joyful appreciation. Those who most strenuously opposed her leaving the School in 1923 later rejoiced that she had followed the dictates of her heart. After a few years Tom transferred to South Carolina, where he continued road building. They had only eight happy years together before his sudden death of a heart attack in 1931.

Well in advance of the close of the session in 1922, Mrs. McLure had made up her mind. In order to give the General Board and the Union adequate time to fill the position, she told Mrs. Eager of her plan to retire at the end of the next session. Mrs. Eager could not believe it. She reasoned, she persuaded, but she made no headway. She then decided that Mrs. McLure was tired; the beloved principal had not had a year off during the arduous fifteen years, for certainly the year of war work was not a year off. So Mrs. Eager tried a new approach. She led the General Board to grant her a year's leave of absence with full salary for the 1923–1924 session.

Doubtless, few of the Board knew at that time the momentous issue at stake. Shortly after the opening of the session, Mrs. Eager began to sound out Mrs. McLure, hoping against hope that the prospect of a year off had changed her mind, but to her dismay she found that the decision was definite, unchanged, and apparently unchangeable. Mrs. McLure was leaving the School.

When the last vestige of hope of retaining Mrs. McLure faded, Mrs. James appointed a committee composed of herself and Miss Mallory; Mrs. Eager, Mrs. Woody, and Mrs. Whayne, from the local Board; and Mrs. George E. Davis, of South Carolina, and Mrs. B. W. Blount, of Florida, from the Board of Trustees, to secure a successor to Mrs. McLure. Mrs. Eager reported at the annual session that much prayer and thought had been given by the committee to the matter, that they had thought the goal was in sight more than once, but as yet they had no definite recommendation. In the emergency, however, Mrs. Eager asked "that the local Board be authorized to make

Miss Carrie Littlejohn acting principal until the position can be filled and give her a helper at Good Will Center."

This was an amazing plan, since the young woman in question, then serving as director of the Good Will Center, had not been consulted. When Mrs. Eager returned, therefore, and announced to her the plan that had been approved for the immediate future, to say she was aghast is putting it mildly! To Mrs. Eager it was not strange at all. She was accustomed to having people co-operate with her plans, and certainly one of her Training School girls could not refuse to help out in such an emergency. This Training School girl at that stage was no match for Mrs. Eager, so, like a pawn of fate or circumstance, she faced her uncertain future.

The session had closed shortly before the Convention with the all-time record class of fifty-nine graduates. The commencement speaker, who was being studied for the position as principal, became seriously ill, and Mrs. McLure had to fill in on short notice.

She had loved her own service flag during the war, and toward the last weeks of the session Miss Coombs, the nurse, had helped her make a large service flag for the School.

The flag was designed in the School colors, with a cross of gold on a field of purple. The individual stars on the lower part of the flag represented the young women who had gone into foreign service. The two large groups of stars at the top suggested the many types of service being done by former students at home. Mrs. McLure made the flag and all that it symbolized the subject of her final address as head of the School.

Shortly after the Convention, a beautiful banquet in honor of Mrs. McLure was given at the School by the local Board. Miss Warren served a wonderful dinner, and under her direction the dining room was turned into a fairyland of gold and purple.

Next to the guest of honor sat her handsome son, looking on and listening with pardonable pride as the speakers paid tribute to his queenly mother. Mrs. Eager welcomed the guests, and Mrs. Whayne acted as toastmistress. Mrs. Woody presented to the School a portrait of Mrs. McLure, a gift from Mrs. Eager and herself. Dr. John Little of the Presbyterian Mission discussed Mrs. McLure's contribution to the religious life of the city. Dr. Mullins, rising to the height of world outlook, spoke eloquently of Mrs. McLure's outreach and impress through her girls on the Baptists of the world.

The Alumnae Association, as their parting gift to their beloved principal, sent her to the Baptist World Alliance in Stockholm in July.

Interim

On arriving home from her trip to Europe, Mrs. McLure graciously consented to return for a few days to help with the opening. There was only a slight falling off in enrolment over the year before, much to the relief of the acting principal, who had feared that the bottom might fall out.

The students of the next two years were as fine as the School has ever enrolled. They were, on the whole, a mature group, but even the youngest were co-operative and mature in their response. In later years six of these students served most acceptably on the faculty and staff, six served on the Board of Trustees, twelve went out as foreign missionaries, eleven served through Woman's Missionary Union channels, and many others did a variety of things in church and social work.

The next year Mrs. Eager reported:

The session of 1924–25, in spite of most strenuous efforts on the part of the committee to secure a successor to Mrs. McLure, opened without this being accomplished. As always, God supplied our needs and Miss Carrie U. Littlejohn graciously consented to serve again in the capacity of principal pro tem.[2]

Enlargement plans for the Good Will Center began in the 1922–1923 session with the purchase of the adjoining property for $5,300. Two years later the erection of a model building on the original lot on Madison Street was authorized, and plans for building began immediately. The double lot provided adequate room for the new building and a small playground. By the fall of 1925 the building was completed at a cost of about $31,000. The larger plant provided much better facilities for practical mission work. Mr. Frank Short, the husband of one of the School's valuable Board members, was the contractor.

Foreign Students

Foreign students began enrolling in the School during this decade of changing conditions and circumstances. They made a definite contribution to the changing pattern of life in the School as they brought to the American student a new awareness of the needs and opportunities in world service. One of the first of these students was Lucy Yao, from Chinkiang, China. She spoke very little English when she first came to the United States, but she could read, so she memorized her way through her classes in typical Chinese style.

Extremely short dresses were in vogue during her stay in Louisville. Mrs. McLure did not feel that it was in good taste for Training School students to adopt such extreme styles, so she warned the girls in student meeting against this unbecoming mode of dress. There was always a question as to how much of any talk, class discussion, or lecture Lucy really understood. Her fellow students soon learned that very little escaped her! For instance, one day she got on a streetcar with another student. At the next corner a sophisticated young woman in a very short dress took a seat diagonally across from them. Lucy observed her seriously for a moment, then turning to her friend she said, "Mrs. McLure, see her, she get *mad!*"

Lucy returned to her country and worked among her own people until the war with Japan. A missionary reported that she was among thousands of Chinese who attempted the long journey on foot toward Chungking and freedom. Disease and exertion took its toll, and she died on the march.

When the delegation from the South went to the Baptist World Congress in Stockholm in 1923, they toured Hungary and Romania, where they found many Baptists who had come to appreciate Southern Baptists because of the material aid sent them after World War I.

One young girl, Ludovica Cristea, heard Dr. Mullins speak in her country in 1920. Standing in the back of the hall as he spoke, she began speaking, unannounced, when he sat down and dramatically made her way through the crowded aisle until she stood before him. She continued the story of her conversion, of the days she had spent in jail because of her love for Christ, and of her gratitude that she was counted worthy to suffer for him. She had been deeply stirred by Dr. Mullins' message, and from that moment she set her heart on going to America to learn more of Christ and the Book that revealed him.

Southern Baptist tourists found her to be as dynamic in 1923 as she had been in 1920. So they pooled their resources and planned for her and another Romanian, Sofia Palyo, to come to the United States and study in Louisville. When these girls arrived in November, 1923, they knew no English that could be understood; communication depended on smiles, head-shaking, eyebrow-lifting, and excited gesticulating, especially on the part of the Romanians. Some of the girls readily offered their services as tutors, and the English lessons began.

War had taken its toll, however, and almost immediately both girls became ill. It was discovered that Ludovica had tuberculosis. The school physician put the case before the County Board of Health and, in fine generosity, they admitted her to the county tuberculosis sanatorium, where she remained for a year. At the end of that time, she was still not pronounced cured, and arrangements were made for her to go to the Southern Baptist Sanatorium in El Paso.

For the long train trip Miss Warren packed a box of lunch. She had found it very difficult to fix food that these girls liked.

Except for onions, Ludovica had never waxed enthusiastic over American food. Into the box of carefully planned delicacies, therefore, Miss Warren sought to please the ailing girl by including two well-wrapped onions. With natural curiosity, Ludovica investigated the box, which had been placed with the rest of her baggage. Picking out the choice tidbits, she hurried to the kitchen, saying in her quaint English, "Thank you, Miss Warren, but I cannot take these onions on American train. Americans say, 'Out, out!'"

After a year in El Paso, American friends sent her back to her country with a prayer that the ministry of Christian hospitals had revealed more to her of the love and compassion of Christ than she could have ever learned in the classroom.

Miss Palyo was under medical care during her first year at the School, for there was no place to send her. Arrangements were made for her to spend the summer at Ridgecrest. She returned to School somewhat improved, but after a second year's trial it became evident that she was in no sense of the word equipped to study in such a school. She refused to return to her country, and who would blame her? She went to visit some Romanian friends in New York and under their guidance learned to make her way in this country.

Kathe and Amalia Gerwich, German Hungarians, also met Southern Baptists in 1923 and appealed to them for a chance to study in Louisville. They were attractive girls from a good German Baptist family. Their zeal and hunger for training touched the hearts of the women in particular, and plans were made for them to come over in 1924. They, too, were suffering from malnutrition. Under medical care and with good food, Amalia improved and returned home in 1927 in good health. Kathe's trouble, however, had gone too far, and a year after she went back to Hungary she passed away.

They knew more English than the Romanian girls, but still they had difficulty, especially in doing the outside reading assigned in most of the courses. One day one of Amalia's teachers asked her how she was getting along. With a troubled expression she said that she did not have time to do all the reading. In an effort to be helpful, the teacher said, "Don't worry about that. Your teachers do not expect you to read all those long assignments word by word. Just skim over it and get the gist of it. That is all you need to do."

Amalia reported at once to a fellow student, "Miss Leetlejohn said I do not need to worry about all thees reading. All I need to do is get the geest of it. If someone will tell me how to get the geest, I will be glad."

Soon after her return, Amalia married a Baptist pastor, and together they worked among their struggling fellow Baptists. It has been difficult for her friends to hear from her since Hungary went behind the Iron Curtain.

One of the most satisfactory foreign students ever to enrol in the Training School was Miss Wu Ming Yung, who came over from Shanghai during the third decade. A third generation Christian, she had a rich background of Christian home life. After graduation from Ginling College in 1923, she had taught in mission schools in Shanghai and shared in the fine fellowship of service in old North Gate Baptist Church. This maturity of attitude and experience prepared her for study in the Training School. She was so well balanced in her thinking that it was impossible for American people to spoil her. Soon after her return to Shanghai in 1934 she was married to S. U. Zau, a fine Christian businessman in Shanghai, and together they have carried on their Christian ministry.

The New Principal

For a year Mrs. Eager and her special committee searched without success throughout the bounds of the Southern Baptist Convention for a successor to Mrs. McLure. Then one day in the early fall of 1924 their attention was directed to a Louisville woman who was known and loved throughout the South, especially in Woman's Missionary Union work. Like the man in the story who searched the world over for diamonds and then returned to find acres of them in his own fields, they found in Mrs. Janie Cree Bose, the beloved corresponding secretary of the Woman's Missionary Union of Kentucky, the answer to their search.

It took a great deal of persuading on Mrs. Eager's part to bring Mrs. Bose to see eye-to-eye with the committee, but Mrs. Eager was a past master in this art. Finding in earnest prayer God's answer, Mrs. Bose allowed her name to be presented to the committee. At a called meeting in Louisville in December she was nominated, and the following May, 1925, she was elected to the office of principal.

Even before her official election she was presented to the school on May 4, 1925, as the commencement speaker. Miss Robbie Trent, in writing of the program in *Royal Service*, said:

. . . Mrs. George B. Eager, chairman of the local Board of Managers, introduced Mrs. Janie Cree Bose, the new principal who will take active direction of the school on August 1. In well chosen words she welcomed Mrs. Bose who has so wonderfully led the W.M.U. of Kentucky for nine years. Her service in her own state and throughout the south during the 75-Million Campaign has meant much to the ongoing of the Master's Kingdom. In her new position, for which she is beautifully fitted, she will go on to even greater influence and service.[3]

Mrs. Bose, a widow with a small son, began her work with the denomination in 1913 as office secretary for Kentucky Woman's Missionary Union. In 1916, when the office of corresponding secretary became vacant, she was promoted then to that position. She served with distinction until 1925. Because of her ability as a speaker, Woman's Missionary Union asked the Kentucky Woman's Missionary Union to give her a leave of absence so that she might serve as the Seventy-five Million Campaign worker throughout the Convention territory.

Mrs. Bose had a very interesting family background of Scottish Presbyterian stock. Her father was a Baptist minister, and her brother, Dr. A. C. Cree, was a leader in Southern Baptist work for many years. The family moved from Scotland to London, where little Janie Cree was born. A few years later they came to this country and settled in North Carolina.

Her first and greatest teacher was her father. After grade school in private schools, she attended Oxford Seminary in North Carolina and Limestone College in South Carolina. Then her family moved to Louisville, giving her the opportunity to become acquainted with the state where she was to do her greatest work.

Memphis, 1925, was not only a milestone for Mrs. Bose but also for Mrs. W. J. Cox. Mrs. James resigned as president of Woman's Missionary Union after nine years of exceptional service. The Union was grieved to give up this beloved leader and dismayed at the thought of finding someone worthy to follow her. Earnest prayers were made for divine wisdom and guidance, and the prayers were answered in the election of Mrs. W. J. Cox, president of Tennessee WMU. With her radiant personality, deep spiritual qualities, and unusual speaking and writing ability, she was God's gift to the Union for the difficult years ahead.

The Parting of the Ways

One of the first problems that the new principal had to face was the adjustment of classes made necessary by the removal of the Seminary to its new location, "The Beeches." It was not a sudden problem, for a tentative plan had been worked out shortly after the war was over when the Seminary began to look to the future. Dr. Mullins had assured the management of the School at that time that Seminary classes could be given in Training School classrooms, provided help would be given the Seminary to enlarge its faculty.

In the meantime, the Seminary had sold the site on Brownsboro Road and bought a much more desirable location on Lexington Road. In the campaign for funds in 1924 the Training School family made a 100 per cent subscription amounting to more than $2,500.

Although the basic buildings were still in an unfinished state, the Seminary moved in March, 1926. Dr. Mullins felt that it would lift the morale of the student body if they could be established on the new campus before the end of the session. It would also give a boost to the campaign for funds to report at the Convention that the Seminary was actually in its new location.

For the few weeks remaining of the session, after the Seminary moved to "The Beeches," a bus transported the girls to the Seminary each day for classes. The bus was old and dilapidated, and the driver never knew whether or not it would make the round trip, but it usually did. Whether they got to classes on time or back to the School for lunch didn't worry the girls particularly. The situation did provide some headaches for Miss Warren in getting the meals served and the dishes washed.

For the next session special provision had to be made for Old and New Testament classes, since the Seminary professors, Dr. John R. Sampey and Dr. A. T. Robertson, had too much work to take on the extra teaching. Dr. C. L. McGinty of Mercer University was elected as Bible teacher for the Training School.

The other Seminary professors, including Dr. Carver, Dr. Dobbins, Dr. Powell, Dr. Adams, and Dr. Tribble, agreed to come to the School to teach their classes. Dr. Sampey and Dr. Robertson very graciously promised that they would come for an occasional lecture when it was possible to arrange for it. It was typical of Dr. Sampey that he returned the honorarium sent him by the School for this service. He had loved the School from the beginning and would accept no remuneration for something he loved to do.

The first floor in the house next door, the Annex, was converted into a classroom now that it was no longer needed for dormitory space. In a year or two life settled down in routine fashion under the new plan. Dr. and Mrs. McGinty were a delightful addition to the Training School family. A new chapter had begun in the life of the School.

One distinct advantage that came out of this change was the smaller classes for the girls. The Seminary classes had by this time become very large. In their own classrooms the girls could ask questions to their heart's content, a privilege that had been denied them at the Seminary except in a few small classes where discussion was possible.

Changes in the Local Board and Faculty

The original Board of the School had been unusually stable. The first major break came when Mrs. McGlothlin moved to Greenville, South Carolina, in 1919 when her husband became president of Furman University.

The great blow came in 1926 when Dr. and Mrs. Eager went to Valdosta, Georgia, to live with their eldest son. Both were failing in health, and it had been evident for some time that they could not continue to carry on even under the protective ministry of the School.

After successful pastorates in Virginia, Tennessee, and Alabama, Dr. Eager had come to the faculty of the Seminary in 1900. Mrs. Eager was at that time in the prime of life, a brilliant, alert woman who was completely happy when she could work for a cause that claimed her loyalty and devotion. Such a cause was the proposed school for training women for missionary service.

For a quarter of a century, beginning and keeping alive the School, persuading Woman's Missionary Union to adopt it, then leading in the movement not only to build its beautiful home at Preston and Broadway but to make it a force in world missions had been the consuming interest of this remarkable woman.

It was fortunate for the School that such a forceful character was in leadership during these strategic years. She had served as co-chairman in the years of maintaining the home for women students, 1904–1907, and continued that relationship for one year after the adoption by Woman's Missionary Union. In 1908 Mrs. Woody insisted that she become chairman of the local Board of Managers, and for eighteen years she continued to direct the activities of the Board and to present the beloved cause in spoken and written message. She often said that she carried the Eager boys (husband and three sons) in the medallion over her heart and the Training School on her back.

Mrs. Woody was there now with more leisure to step capably and graciously back into the office of chairman, and the shock of Mrs. Eager's going was cushioned.

Miss Eliza Broadus, who had called the Louisville women together in 1904 to consider establishing a home for the young women coming to study in the Seminary, had served continuously on the Board. Now, because of advanced years and increasing deafness, she retired from its membership. Mrs. W. J. Druien, who had also served since the "little home" years, resigned because of removal from the city.

Another generation of strong women had been raised up to step into service. For instance, Mrs. Frank Short came on the Board in 1922 and continued to use her keen business mind and practical common sense in the interest of the School until 1953.

Other members who came on the Board about the same time and served for about fifteen years were Mrs. E. B. Robertson, Mrs. W. P. Hall, Mrs. J. M. Delph, and Mrs. E. T. Farmer. In 1927 Mrs. John R. Sampey, Miss Jennie Graham Bright, Miss Latta Greer, and Mrs. Richard Bean were elected to membership and continued to serve until the local Board was merged with the Board of Trustees ten years later.

Miss Greer succeeded Mrs. Eager as treasurer and gave the School the benefit of her fine business ability until Woman's

Missionary Union changed the plan of handling the School's funds. Mrs. Sampey was retained as a resident member of the Board of Trustees until her removal from the city in 1947. Her contribution was a fitting supplement to that of her distinguished husband, who was a true friend and helper from its beginning until death ended his long career as professor and president of the Seminary.

During this decade the missionary education course began to develop from a simple course in mission study into a Woman's Missionary Union methods course. Miss Wilma Bucy, of Mississippi, a graduate student, became Mrs. Eager's assistant on a teaching fellowship in 1922. The next year she was elected to the faculty, and in good earnest she began to build up a comprehensive introduction to the broad field of Woman's Missionary Union organizations and methods. Miss Bucy continued to do creative and constructive work in developing the course until 1927 when she went to Tennessee as Woman's Missionary Union field worker.

Miss Hannah Reynolds, the Young People's secretary in Alabama, succeeded Miss Bucy. After one year, illness in her family made it necessary for her to give up the work. Miss Elsie Ragsdale, who was Woman's Missionary Union field worker in South Carolina, was elected to fill the vacancy.

In 1926 Mrs. E. A. McDowell was secured to teach music, and she continued on the faculty while her husband was a student at the Seminary. The following year Miss Claudia Edwards was elected as assistant in music.

A Year of Remembrance

Women, as a rule, never miss an opportunity to celebrate an anniversary, and Southern Baptist women are no exception. In 1927 Woman's Missionary Union leadership and the General Board of the Training School joined forces to observe the twentieth anniversary of the School.

It happened that the Southern Baptist Convention and

101

Woman's Missionary Union were both having their annual meetings in Louisville that year. The first evening session of Woman's Missionary Union, meeting in the Warren Memorial Presbyterian Church, was given over to the School's commencement exercises. A great host of the alumnae made this occasion a home-coming that surpassed that of 1918 when the new building was dedicated. Joining the student body in the familiar processional, they provided a memorable experience for the delegates and visitors, many of whom were having their first opportunity to see the School.

Mrs. Eager was having her first visit in Louisville after two years' absence. In choice words of reminiscence and appreciation she presented the speaker, Mrs. McLure, who was also having her first official visit since her retirement four years ago.

Under the subject, "High Lights of Twenty Years," Mrs. McLure pointed up the School's remarkable progress in a series of word pictures that clearly indicated the School's unique contribution to the missionary purpose of the Union. The beloved Dr. Eager and Miss Leachman were back for this great occasion, too, and gave the "old-timers" an added reason for feeling at home as the two friends shared in the program by giving the invocation and leading in the closing prayer.

Mrs. Bose and Miss Warren arranged for the Alumnae Association to have its dinner in the beautiful dining room of the School. The china that had been the special gift of friends during this twentieth anniversary was christened at the banquet. Miss Warren's table decorations made the occasion beautiful.

One little "slip-up" spoiled the dinner and hurt Miss Warren's pride and goal of perfection where special dinners were concerned. Being a great lover of coffee, she made every effort to teach the girls to serve only the best on ordinary as well as special occasions. On the other hand, she was economical where the School was concerned and taught the girls that a small pitcher of coffee left over from one meal could be safely used again without spoiling the fresh supply.

Miss Carrie U. Littlejohn
Principal and President, 1931–1951

Mrs. Maud Reynolds McLure
Principal
1907–1923

Mrs. J. H. Anderson
(Mrs. Janie Cree Bose)
Principal, 1925–1930

Miss Emily Lansdell
President, 1951–1958

Dr. William Owen Carver

Now, that afternoon the School had held open house for the delegates and visitors. Gallons of fruit punch had been served. When the last guest departed, a pitcher of punch was brought back to the serving room and left on the counter near the coffee urn. Alas and alack! The girl designated to make the coffee that evening gave one look at the pitcher and from habit dumped it into the urn.

At the dinner that evening some former students tasted their coffee and wondered curiously what had happened to Training School coffee. In a moment Miss Warren tasted the coffee. One taste was enough! She left her table quickly and marched with an injured air across the dining room to the serving room. When she found what had happened, she emptied the urn and made a fresh supply of coffee. She sent the serving girls out to collect the punch-flavored variety, and in a short time they returned with the kind for which Miss Warren was famous.

The Passing of Dr. Mullins

The last great change that came to the Training School during this period was the death of Dr. Mullins. In November, 1928, he passed away in his sixty-eighth year after an extended illness.

Dr. Mullins became president of the Southern Baptist Seminary in 1899, just a few months before Dr. Simmons started the agitation about a woman's missionary training school. If a man without his broad vision and progressive ideas had been at the helm of the Seminary at the turn of the century, one wonders what would have been the fate of Dr. Simmons' idea.

By birth, education, and experience he was prepared for the tremendous task of leadership upon which he entered in Southern Baptist life. Born in Mississippi, brought up and educated in Texas, trained for ministerial work at the Southern Baptist Seminary, experienced in pastoral work, first in a small town in Kentucky, then in Baltimore, and finally in the cultural town of Newton Center, Massachusetts, Dr. Mullins had a broad understanding of the entire territory of the Convention.

Though he was a very busy man, he gave his interest, his time, and his best thought to the beginning of a project designed to help young women of our denomination receive the specialized missionary training that they needed. With his background, he was not inhibited by the conservatism that made the majority of Southern Baptists of that era slow to embrace new ideas and ways of doing things. From the beginning he felt that a training school was a project for Woman's Missionary Union. The Seminary would co-operate in every possible way, but a responsible organization should manage and direct its affairs as an institution independent of the Seminary.

His contribution to the Training School was priceless. While the Louisville women were trying to work out their strategy in 1905 to get the proposed school on the Woman's Missionary Union annual program, they went to Dr. Mullins for advice. All through the difficult three years he encouraged and guided them. When the Union adopted the School in 1907, he helped prepare the formal resolutions that were necessary to transfer ownership. No important step was ever taken without conference with him. When Mrs. McLure was leaving the School in 1923, she spoke of Dr. Mullins as her big brother who had helped her through many difficult situations.

Dr. Mullins had been in on all the great occasions. He presided and spoke at the inaugural program in 1907. At the laying of the cornerstone in 1917 he said something that was often quoted in those building years: "The Training School is a prayer, 'Thy kingdom come,' that is answering itself." He added his word of greeting and congratulations at the dedication in 1918.

Perhaps the most memorable contacts with him came at Christmas when caroling took the Training School family to his home, or when he and Mrs. Mullins came to have Christmas dinner at the School. He seemed to enjoy this close touch with the girls, and those who were lucky enough to be seated at the guest table could never forget the stimulating conversation. They knew they had been close to greatness that day.

The Christmas greeting he sent to the School in 1920 has been preserved in the scrapbook. It was not a formal card but one composed and written on an ordinary correspondence card. What an extraordinary message it was!

GREETINGS TO THE WOMAN'S MISSIONARY UNION TRAINING SCHOOL:

You live in the House Beautiful on the corner of Preston and Broadway, near the heart of a great city. We love to think of you at this Christmas season as living close to the heart of God on the corner of two great highways, one leading along the Twentieth Century with all its sorrow and sin and need, the other leading from Time to the sunlit hills of Eternity, made radiant all the way by the Gospel of Christ.

The House Beautiful enshrines a beautiful thought which has crystallized into many beautiful purposes, expressed in many consecrated lives. As Jesus lay in the Manger two thousand years ago as a little babe, the Bearer of divine grace, so each of your lives is a new incarnation of that grace for the blessing of the world.

We send you our greetings and our love and express our joy at the blessing for others which impends in your preparation for service.

Wishing the fulness of Christmas peace and joy to every member of the Faculty, the Executive Committee and the Student body, we are

Yours in the Master's Service,

E. Y. MULLINS
ISLA MAY MULLINS

LOUISVILLE, KY.
Dec. 25, 1920

The School had been tested with drastic changes during these ten years. Were the foundations that were laid lasting foundations? Was the inner life built on sand or rock? Could the School survive now that so many who shaped its future had thrown the torch to other hands? Three decades of continuous service through sunshine and shadow give the answer.

4

The Stimulus of Difficulty

What is difficulty?—Only a word indicating the
degree of strength requisite for accomplishing
particular objects; a mere notice of the necessity
for exertion; a bugbear to children and fools;
only a stimulus to men.—SAMUEL WARREN

IF THE PRECEDING DECADE was haunted by the specter of
change, this one—1927 through 1937—was harassed by a
chain of difficulties. The problem of enrolment began in the
early twenties. Established in the spacious new building and
free at last from the shadow of war, under the impact of the
Seventy-five Million Campaign the enrolment suddenly began
to rise. By 1921 there were 142 students crowded into the
dormitory designed to house only 117 girls comfortably. Under
such conditions the management began to make immediate
plans for enlargement. Fortunately, the recession, if it had to
come, came in time to forestall the actual enlargement of the
building on the corner of Preston and Broadway in downtown
Louisville.

Enrolment

Beginning with a gradual decrease in enrolment, there was
a sudden drop in 1926 to seventy-nine boarding students. For
the next five years the boarding group stabilized at an average
of eighty-one. A gradual decrease started again, and by 1934
there were only fifty-four girls in the dormitory. The day students continued to attend in large numbers. Men at the Semi-

nary, even those who were married, could manage to work enough on the side to make their way.

The major reason, of course, for the falling off in enrolment was the increasing difficulty the students found in getting into the work for which they were being prepared. The Foreign Mission Board began having financial problems shortly after the Seventy-five Million Campaign. As a result, very few Training School graduates were appointed to foreign service for several years. The Home Board and other church agencies were facing similar hardships.

Placement Problems

One of the first problems to which Mrs. Bose applied her energies as she began her work as principal in 1925 was finding work for the girls as they left the School. If they could not get into their chosen field of missions, was there some other church vocation toward which they could turn? Pastors had been talking and writing to Mrs. Bose about the need for trained women in the local church field. As a trial in that direction, she introduced into the curriculum in 1925 a course for church secretaries.

At the suggestion of Dr. Dobbins, the Sunday School Board made it possible for him to offer a course in Christian education to Training School students. This course, giving the fundamentals of a program of religious education in the church along with the course in typing and shorthand, prepared several good maid-of-all-work church secretaries. The secretarial course as such lost its popularity after the first two years and apparently was dropped after four years, though typing continued to be taught spasmodically for several years. Dr. Dobbins continued his course in the practical aspects of the church field as long as the School remained downtown.

During this period, depression, circumstances, and necessary adjustment to changing conditions forced the School to start to drift away from its original purpose of training women for efficient service in foreign, home, and city missions. At the same time, it began to play up its minor purpose of training church and Sunday school workers in an effort to enlist students and prepare them for whatever doors of service were open. In this way the investment in the building could be used to advantage for the good of the denomination.

Throughout these years of difficulty the Woman's Missionary Union forces, both Southwide and state, tried valiantly to help place the students in some form of service. They provided the first opportunities for summer work with no remuneration except expenses and experience. They urged associations and rural areas to employ the girls, who welcomed every open door to service regardless of the little or no salary that might go along with it.

As times grew worse in the early thirties, new interpretations were put upon religious work. Why should we not look upon every vocation as sacred? Had the Christian world overemphasized the separation of the sacred and secular? And so teachers sought to satisfy the urge of that generation of dedicated young women by pointing out to them the Christian opportunities in the schoolroom and in the business office.

Financial Difficulties

The difficulties of this decade were so enmeshed and related that it is hard to say what was cause and what was effect. The over-all trouble, of course, was financial; money was not easily obtained. This problem caused a chain reaction in the School's program. It cut down the enrolment and thereby caused a more acute financial situation in the School. The overhead expense had to go on regardless of the size of the student body, but one source of the current expense fund, student board, was cut nearly 40 per cent by 1934. The contribution from the Cooperative Program, which in 1928 was over $15,000, dropped steadily to its lowest point, $2,786 in 1933.

To live within its income the School was forced to make drastic cuts in the current expense fund. The financial problem became more involved in 1930 when the Louisville Trust Company closed with over $7,000 of the School's funds. Fortunately, through the years an emergency fund had accumulated. The management had been trained under Mrs. Eager's ideas of economy not only to live within the School's income but also to close the year always with a balance. This policy enabled the School to meet its financial crises without going into debt.

Out of Their Poverty

One of the bright pictures against this background of financial trials was the joyous abandon that prompted the students of this period to give to the special offerings of the Union. Most of the girls had little spending money. Many had nothing beyond the scholarship that was designed to cover board and books. Yet they managed always to come up with an amount that would put to shame the average church group. For instance, during the 1925–1926 session students and resident faculty together gave to the Seminary building fund and the December and March special offerings a total of over $3,900.

In 1928, when Woman's Missionary Union was celebrating its Ruby Anniversary year, the students prayed and worked for an offering of $1,000. They gave a total of $1,093, which they inscribed in the Kentucky Woman's Missionary Union Memory Book as a tribute to their beloved principal, Mrs. Bose, who had led them to such heights of missionary zeal.

In the 1930–1931 session, with personal funds almost non-existent, they made a Christmas offering for foreign missions of $880.50, and in March a home mission offering of $226.95. Paul gave the only explanation for such cheerful giving in the memorable words, "Their overflowing joy and their deep poverty together have poured out a flood of rich generosity" (2 Cor. 8:2, Moffatt).

The School Loses Its Principal

Shortly after the Southern Baptist Convention of 1930 the Training School board and faculty members became conscious of an undercurrent of excitement and mystery. Mrs. Woody returned from the Woman's Missionary Union annual meeting with the air of a woman who knows something but is not yet ready to talk. She was in and out of the building all day long. She went on shopping trips, and boxes and bundles began to arrive. The staff members observed and talked among themselves. Board members exchanged confidences. Something was going on, but nobody knew an explanation.

Finally, the news came out. On June 10, 1930, Mrs. Janie Cree Bose was married to James H. Anderson, of Knoxville, Tennessee. They had known each other for several years in a casual way. Mr. Anderson had been thinking of her in a more than casual way for a long time. When he learned that she was planning to go on a mission tour with Miss Mallory to South America that summer, and continue her work indefinitely in the School, he decided that life was too short for their chance at happiness to be longer delayed. With gentle persuasion, and yet with something of the forceful ability that had made him one of the most successful businessmen among Southern Baptists, he convinced her that his plan was better than hers.

The affection of Southern Baptists for these two wonderful people was reflected in the press notices. The reaction of the *Religious Herald* of Virginia was typical: "On June 10, . . . in Louisville, Ky., Mrs. Janie Cree Bose, . . . greatly beloved in Virginia, was married to Mr. James H. Anderson, of Knoxville, Tenn. . . . No more useful Southern Baptists live than Mr. and Mrs. Anderson and their friends will wish for them many happy years in their united life." [1]

During the preceding year, Miss Littlejohn had enjoyed a sabbatical leave for study in the Hartford School of Religious Education in Connecticut. At the close of the school year she had gone up into New Hampshire on a vacation with a group of friends. They had the use of a cottage on a beautiful lake near New London. One cold, rainy day they were enjoying an open fire when someone came in with the mail. A letter for her from Louisville naturally was opened first. The news was so startling that one of the group, looking at her, asked with concern, "Have you had bad news?"

Not wishing to explain the fear that clutched her heart, she replied, "No, just amazing news!"

In a few days she met Mrs. Woody in New York, and together they saw Mr. and Mrs. Anderson off to Europe. On observing their radiant happiness, how could the former acting principal regret the step they had taken, even though it brought the old responsibility back to her?

As she had feared, Mrs. Woody brought the news that the Board wanted her to take over again as acting principal. Under the circumstances she could not refuse. There seemed to be no one else immediately available. So she turned away from a stimulating year of study and a perfect vacation and faced again the new, old task in Louisville.

What a year that was! A small student body, though not as small as it would be a year or two later; students getting along on a shoestring, but giving joyously and generously out of their meager funds; banks closed and no money on which to operate except the precious emergency fund; small salaries that had to be cut in order to live within the School's income. It was well that those responsible for the School did not know that this was not the hardest year. A loyal faculty and staff accepted their difficulties in fine spirit.

In March, 1931, the special committee, composed of Mrs. W. J. Cox, president of Woman's Missionary Union; Miss Juliette Mather, representing the alumnae; Mrs. J. L. Johnson, of Mississippi, and Mrs. George E. Davis, of South Carolina, representing the Board of Trustees, met in Louisville and nominated Miss Littlejohn as principal. In May at the annual session of Woman's Missionary Union in Birmingham she was elected to that position.

In accepting this high office, the new principal said to the constituency through the pages of *Royal Service:*

> On this opening day of our twenty-fifth anniversary year I am reminded that I am beginning my first year of service as the principal of the W.M.U. Training School, though it is my eleventh year of work with the school in some official capacity.
>
> You have asked me to undertake a hard task. It is particularly difficult at a time like this when so few doors of service are open to our graduates, because of current conditions. It is difficult, too, because it is a transitional period for the school. . . . I am grateful for its sure foundations in the plan of God and I pledge my full cooperation in preserving its ideals and standards and distinctive atmosphere. My co-workers are one with me in their desire to adjust the program to the needs of the day without sacrificing those intangible qualities that have made the school a rare blessing to hundreds of students and visitors through the twenty-four years of its history.[2]

Raising Educational Standards

One of the first problems to which the faculty gave its attention in the fall of 1930 was a study of degrees and corresponding requirements. This study of standards was no sudden spurt of educational or intellectual ambition but was in line with a policy of growth established in the early days.

After thorough consideration, the faculty recommended to the Board of Trustees that the School discontinue the degrees of Bachelor and Master of Missionary Training and substitute the degrees that had become standard in the field of religious education, Bachelor and Master of Religious Education.

In setting up the necessary requirements for the new degrees, standardized procedures were followed: the candidate for the Bachelor of Religious Education degree must have had two years of basic college work and must have completed sixty semester hours in the Training School. The candidate for the Master of Religious Education degree must have a bachelor's degree in arts, science, or religious education and must spend two years in resident graduate study.

Other Losses

There are losses and gains of human resources in the life of an institution that are far more important than those in the financial realm. It was inevitable in the passing years that, one by one, the original local Board members would drop out of active service. Mrs. Woody resigned as chairman of the local Board and went to Europe in the summer of 1931 for an indefinite stay. Her stimulating presence and wise leadership were missed in the Board's deliberations.

Miss Eliza Broadus, another member of the original Board, had resigned because of increasing deafness. Now as she approached her eightieth birthday plans were in the making to honor her with a luncheon at the Training School on October 1. Miss Mallory enlisted the Woman's Missionary Union Executive Committee, the Kentucky Woman's Missionary Union Executive Committee, the local Board of Managers, and the Training School alumnae in the delightful project. Each of these groups had abundant reason to appreciate this lovely woman.

When Woman's Missionary Union was organized in 1888, Miss Broadus was elected vice-president from Kentucky. Even before that date she had become the beloved leader of Kentucky Baptist women. She had taken the initial step in providing a home for the young women studying at the Seminary in 1904. Naturally she was among the charter members of the original Board of Managers of the new home. In view of her long and constructive service, her friends wanted to make this birthday a happy one for her.

As a pretext to get her to come to the School on the given day, she was asked to tell the students about her father's work on his *Commentary on the Gospel of Matthew*. Her sister, Mrs. A. T. Robertson, was in on the secret, and she took pride in seeing that Miss Broadus was dressed in a new outfit, though both dress and hat were as quaint as her previous models.

With childlike animation, she told of her father's work on the book through twenty years, of the help from all his children, especially the eldest daughter, for this project preceded the day of typewriters and stenographers. Of special interest was her account of the most recent translation of the book into another foreign language. A missionary in Mexico, Miss Sarah Hale, had translated the commentary into Spanish and published it at her own expense. Miss Broadus' missionary heart rejoiced that through her father's books he could continue to have a part in the ongoing business of missions.

When Miss Broadus had finished her story, Mrs. Whayne arose and began to make a speech about Miss Broadus, introducing it with some lines in verse written especially for this occasion by Miss Margaret Lackey, of Mississippi.

Mrs. Robertson cleverly explained later that Miss Broadus' "imperfect hearing came to the relief of her modesty," so she was not embarrassed as Mrs. Whayne continued to bring the tribute of many hearts. As a token of love and appreciation from her many friends, a tall loving cup filled with actual gold pieces was placed in her hands. With naive astonishment she exclaimed, "Why, there is something in it!"

It was a happy day for her, and friends liked to remember her as they saw her that day. Just one week later, as she went to the mailbox one block from her home, she was struck down by a large truck and instantly killed.

Miss Eliza S. Broadus was the eldest daughter of Dr. John A. Broadus, one of the founders and the second president of the Southern Baptist Theological Seminary. She was born in Charlottesville, Virginia, while her father was chaplain of the University, and grew up in Greenville, South Carolina. When the Seminary was moved to Louisville in 1877, she was a mature young woman, well educated under her father's supervision and already his able assistant.

After the death of her father and stepmother, she made her home with her halfsister, Mrs. A. T. Robertson. Never was an in-law more beloved and wanted than Miss Broadus, who was "Sister" to Dr. and Mrs. Robertson and to the Robertson children. Mrs. Robertson was particularly proud of the fact that Miss Broadus could trace her lineage through her mother right back to George Washington. Once when young Archie Robertson was rude to the beloved "Sister," his mother ended her lecture with, "Don't ever treat Sister like that again! Remember she is kin to George Washington, and you and I are not!"

Miss Mallory's tribute to Miss Broadus in *Royal Service* perhaps more thoroughly epitomized her varied service than anything that has been written about her:

Few southern Baptist women have equalled Miss Eliza S. Broadus in the service rendered her "own generation according to the will of God." Fourscore years and one week were granted to her and she not only used them to help lovingly in the home, church, community and state but for more than half of her life she was a most efficient officer of Woman's Missionary Union. . . .

In living terms one will ever think of Miss Broadus, for she was always so active, alert and animated that death cannot be associated with her.[3]

Gains

In the coming of new life and leadership in the Board of Managers there was some compensation for the severe losses in personnel during this period. For example, Mrs. Woody's retirement as chairman of the local Board brought Mrs. Trevor H. Whayne to the forefront in board leadership. She had been on the original committee in 1904 and continued her service on the local Board without interruption until it was merged with the Board of Trustees in 1937. She was then elected to membership on the Board of Trustees as one of the seven resident members. She loved the School with sincere devotion. A gifted writer, she used her pen often in the early days in putting the School's needs before the constituency.

On Founder's Day a few days after her death in September, 1938, one of her long-time friends and Board members, Mrs. W. J. Druien, paid tribute to her and other members of the original committee.

Several new members, who have been worthy successors to those first devoted women, were added to the local Board at this time: Mrs. E. M. Nuckols, in 1929; Mrs. J. B. Weatherspoon and Miss Margaret Frost, in 1931; and Mrs. George C. Burton, in 1933. After the local Board was merged with the Board of Trustees, Mrs. Nuckols, Mrs. Weatherspoon, and Mrs. Burton were retained among the seven resident members.

Miss Frost (now Mrs. George Roden) continued as a member at large on the Board of Trustees until 1953. It was her privilege thus to conserve the unique contribution made by her distinguished father, Dr. J. M. Frost, who championed the cause of the proposed school in the Southern Baptist Convention and later led the Sunday School Board, of which he was secretary, to give generously to its first and second building campaigns.

Silver Anniversary

During the 1931–1932 session the twenty-fifth anniversary of the School was celebrated. In spite of the depression the year was made memorable. One of the projects of the year was the purchase of flat silver for the dining room. So many small gifts of money came in from societies for the flat silver that there was enough left over to buy a silver service, which has graced innumerable tea tables since that time.

Another feature of the anniversary was the first radio program ever given by the School. The chorus, trained and directed by Miss Claudia Edwards, provided the music, and Miss Littlejohn spoke briefly on the School's history.

The crowning event of the anniversary year was the commencement, when the new degrees were given for the first time. Mrs. McLure delivered the address on the theme, "The Greatness of God." Mrs. James H. Anderson was on the platform to lead in the opening prayer. Mrs. Eager was back for this memorable occasion but did not feel well enough to take any part on the program.

The commencement luncheon was a beautiful occasion. The honor guests were Mrs. McLure, Mrs. Eager, Mr. and Mrs. J. H. Anderson, Miss Mary Pratt, Mrs. Frank Short, Miss Fannie Moses, and Mrs. T. H. Whayne. During the meal students put on an interesting program, featuring "A Board Meeting of 1907," in which they cleverly imitated Mrs. Woody, Mrs. Eager, Mrs. McLure, Mrs. Whayne, and Miss Moses. Mrs. Woody was not present, but she sent a cablegram from Italy.

One of the delayed features of the Silver Anniversary was the history of the first twenty-five years. The committee had counted on Mrs. Woody as the author. She had been on the scene from the beginning, she knew the story from the inside, and now she had the leisure to undertake it. It was November, 1932, before she returned from her extended travels abroad. She refused to undertake the assignment, pleading no gift at writing, but assured the committee that she would secure a writer.

In short order she announced that Mrs. E. Y. Mullins would write the history. Mrs. Woody did all the research and spent many hours with Mrs. Mullins and a stenographer. The history, written in Mrs. Mullins' delightful style and published in 1934, portrays the story as told by one who had an intimate association with its leading characters from the beginning.

Beyond the Shadows

On Mother's Day, May 14, 1933, Mrs. George B. Eager slipped quietly "beyond the shadows into the full, clear light"

117

of the great beyond. It so happened that on that Sunday Miss Warren and Miss Littlejohn met Mrs. Woody at Broadway Baptist Church, had dinner with her, then went to her apartment in the Mayflower Hotel. As they entered the door, the phone was ringing. Mrs. Woody engaged in a brief conversation, then turned to tell her guests with deep emotion of the homegoing of her friend and theirs.

Mrs. Eager's personality had many facets. The portrait of her at the School depicts her in all her queenly bearing, and in her early and middle years she was a queenly woman. In the early years of her work with the School she was the persuasive leader, the keen strategist, the tactful diplomat who handled the difficult situations and wrote the important letters where words must be either weapons or healing agents. During her last years in Louisville she became "Grandmother Eager" to the students. The title seemed to bring out all her innate gentleness and sweetness.

A girlhood friend said to her, on hearing that she was engaged to the young ministerial student, "Don't marry George Eager. You will ruin his life." On the contrary, she was the perfect complement to his ministry as pastor and teacher as she looked after the practical details of life that bothered him not at all. She was a rare combination, a woman of vision far beyond the average, yet one who kept her feet firmly planted on the ground as she sought to bring her visions to reality. The School was fortunate to enlist in its service a woman with such a rich background of culture, insight, ability, and religious experience.

A few days after Mrs. Eager's death Mrs. Woody went to New Jersey to visit her son, Dr. McIver Woody. On June 14, she, too, passed away quietly in her sleep. In a strange but beautiful way life ended almost simultaneously for these two remarkable women. In *Royal Service* underneath their pictures were these words: "Side by side for more than a quarter of a century they led in the movement that established and main-

First Location 1904–1906
Fourth Street near Breckinridge

Second Location 1906–1907
Broadway at Eighth Street

Third Location 1907–1917, 334 East Broadway

WMU Training School 1918–1942, 334 East Broadway

Carver School of Missions and Social Work, 2801 Lexington Road

tained this school dear to the heart of every southern Baptist woman. Almost hand in hand they entered that 'Other Country' to hear their Master say: 'Well done. . . . Enter thou into the joy of thy Lord.' " [4]

Mrs. Woody, as Emma McIver, was born and brought up in Texas, and many of the best qualities of that great state were exemplified in her personality and service. Educated at Baylor College, she was trained for Christian leadership in church and community. She came to Louisville as a bride in 1885 and immediately made for herself a place in church and community affairs. Fifteen years later, when the training school movement started, she was mature and ready for the great service of her life.

Nature was lavish in her gifts to Mrs. Woody. She had the kind of physical beauty that advancing years did not wither. Even more marked than her physical appearance was her magnetic personality. Someone said that when she entered a room, it was as if a light were turned on. To make the combination more remarkable, she had the down-to-earth forthrightness and business ability that bring things to pass. She saw through things quickly, made up her mind without wavering, and when she took over a task it was as good as done.

At the opening of the session in 1933 a memorial service was held for these two great women. Dr. John R. Sampey, president of the Seminary, paid a tribute to Mrs. Eager, and Dr. W. O. Carver to Mrs. Woody.

In connection with the service, Mr. Albert Woody presented to the School a portrait of his mother—a gift from him, his brother Dr. McIver Woody, and his sister Miss Elizabeth Woody.

First Observance of Founder's Day

The observance of Founder's Day was initiated on October 2, 1935. As a matter of fact, in May, 1924, on the suggestion of Mrs. W. C. James, president of Woman's Missionary

Union, the Board of Trustees voted to observe the day annually. Due to changes in administration during the intervening years, the plan was overlooked until 1935.

For this initial observance the School was fortunate in its two speakers, Mrs. McLure and Dr. Carver. The only living member of the five founders, Mrs. McLure told of the School's struggles in its early years and of her valiant co-workers, Miss Broadus, Mrs. Woody, Mrs. Eager, and Miss Heck.

Dr. Carver, as professor of missions in the Southern Baptist Seminary, was pre-eminently fitted to give an over-all picture of the movement. Miss Ethel Winfield, in a summary of his address, said:

As he spoke of the five "chief founders" of the institution he told how the delicate, sensitive soul of Miss Broadus caught the seed dropped by Dr. E. Z. Simmons in 1899 and nurtured it until time was ripe for its fruitbearing; Mrs. Eager he characterized as the "mothering soul of the institution and its defender against criticism." Mrs. S. E. Woody was born for an executive and was in every situation the center of courage, while Miss Heck exercised in the school's behalf her genius for administration. To these four God added a fifth whose spirit He had fitted to become the soul of the institution, Mrs. McLure, "and," said the speaker, "the soul stands after all else has passed on." [5]

Many special guests were present for this first Founder's Day. Among them were Miss Kathleen Mallory, Miss Emma Leachman, ten state trustees, and a number of former students. It was a particularly significant occasion for Miss Elsie Gilliam, of Virginia, and Miss Beulah Bowden, of North Carolina, members of the first student body in 1907.

Life Was Like That

Life was not all gloom during this difficult decade. In fact, the difficulties in life formed a background that more perfectly pointed up the bright spots.

It was as thrilling as a new experience to have Dr. Maddry,

secretary of the Foreign Mission Board, write for a list of the members of the student body who would be ready in the spring of 1937 for appointment for foreign service. Unfortunately, it had been so long since this door had been open that mission volunteers had turned to other vocations.

From the small class of twenty-two graduates in 1936 only three were appointed. This was better, however, than the previous year, when only one of a class of twenty-one was appointed. In 1934, when the Foreign Mission Board presented eight new appointees at the Woman's Missionary Union annual session, three of them were former Training School students.

During the lean years of this period Training School students did some of their most beautiful work. For instance, the summer between her two years in Louisville one of the most attractive, capable, and best prepared of the students worked in the mountains of eastern Kentucky for no remuneration except expenses. In the section where she worked there were no educated ministers. Some of them could not even read, yet the young people in these churches were having the advantage of high school education. Under such circumstances it was difficult to give these boys and girls a higher conception of the Christian faith.

The following May some of these young people made the long trip to Louisville to be present at the graduation of their beloved teacher and friend. She had made such a deep impression on them that they wanted not only to see her but also the School that had helped to make her the kind of person she was.

Amusing as well as inspiring stories mark this period of student life. One young woman from a small town in the deep South had her first experience visiting homes in the slum section of the city. That evening in field work prayer meeting she prayed earnestly for the homes and the people she had seen that afternoon. Finally, in the midst of her prayer she exclaimed, "Lord, you'd be surprised at the conditions you'd find in some of these homes!"

Another girl, a solemn sort of person, prayed most fervently, "Lord, make us fishers of men!" There were some people in the chapel who chose to put the wrong interpretation on the earnest prayer!

Some of the students had difficulty adjusting to the noise of Preston Street. Saturday evenings in particular could be maddening to the poor sleepers when the family feuds or hilarious visiting of foreign-speaking people carried on under their windows far into the night. Late one Saturday night there was a violent ringing of the Preston Street doorbell. Calling a student across the hall to go with her, Miss Warren went to the door and found a very angry Italian and his wife. In highly excited Italian-American, he told her that someone in the building had thrown water on him. She insisted that he was mistaken.

"No one in this building would do anything like that!" she said.

He then showed her his wet hat to prove his point. She tried to calm him, but he became more angry and more excited. Finally, he threatened to sue "this place."

By this time several students had heard the argument and joined the strange assortment in the hall. Finally, Miss Warren asked the man if he would be satisfied if she gave him the money to have his hat cleaned. He grunted something that could have been yes or no. In a moment she brought out fifty cents; he looked at it, turned and discussed the issue with his wife, then took the money and stalked out.

Years later the story came out when the conscientious girl who had thrown the water eased her conscience by telling all! Her roommate, a poor sleeper, endured the noise as long as her frazzled nerves could take it. She hadn't tried this before, but perhaps it would work. Suiting the action to the thought, she got up and got a glass of water. Turning to the innocent little roommate, she said, "Throw it out the window."

Accustomed to letting the senior take the initiative, she did as she was told and made a direct hit! When the noise on the street was brought into the building, the frightened senior made the terrified junior promise never to tell!

Along with the planned fun, there was much that was not planned, and the students were not always the innocent cause of it. As long as the School remained downtown the principal led a brief devotional service at the breakfast table on Sunday mornings. One morning her alarm failed to wake her, and the first thing she heard was a furious pounding on her door. On opening it, she saw a student whose eyes were practically popping out of her head.

"What shall I tell 'em?" the girl exclaimed.

"Tell 'em?" was the puzzled reply.

"Everybody is in the dining room waiting for you!"

That galvanized the lady into action and, picking up a Bible, she told the girl to take it to Miss Ragsdale, asking her to read a passage and have a brief prayer. The girl ran back down the long hall and placed the Bible in the teacher's hand with the whispered request.

Miss Ragsdale took the Bible and by some quirk of fate turned to Psalm 121. When she got to the words, "Behold, he that keepeth Israel shall neither slumber nor sleep," some of the staff members almost had to leave the room! To appreciate that story fully one has to remember how punctiliously dormitory residents in those days went to meals and tried to meet all their responsibilities on time. Being an example was hard on a teacher!

Life was never dull. It was a mixture of stimulating work and fun as well as situations that caused concern and sorrow. Shortly after the session closed in May, 1935, Miss Warren had a serious heart attack which kept her in bed all summer. After a few weeks her doctor advised her to give up the work, as she needed to live quietly for an indefinite period.

She lived in Lexington, Kentucky, until her death in 1945. During these years of enforced leisure she continued to be interested in her church, in the School, and in the students whom she had known and loved.

Mrs. T. H. Whayne said of Miss Warren that "she combined the qualities of efficiency and generalship with the culture and refinement of a true Southern lady." The students loved and respected her. Her co-workers found in her a loyal, congenial friend. The School had her devotion and fifteen years of service rarely equaled.

Fortunately, the School was able to secure Miss Mary Mitchell, who had served in the same position so acceptably from 1914 to 1920. This happy solution of what could have been a serious problem was considered providential.

Another sorrow came to the school in 1935 in the homegoing of Mrs. E. Y. Mullins. A semi-invalid for most of the years she lived in Louisville, she did not let that crush her spirit or prevent her from living a normal life. As first lady at the Seminary she was a perfect hostess, though often she had to have a friend do the honors for her. On such occasions she insisted on greeting her guests in her bedroom upstairs. In addition to being a wonderful helpmeet to her distinguished husband, she was a personage in her own right, a gifted artist and writer. The portrait of her at the School, presented by Dr. and Mrs. H. W. Tribble, was her own work. The last of her more than a dozen books was *House Beautiful,* the history of the School's first twenty-five years.

Founders' Day, 1936

This second observance of Founders' Day was notable because a portrait of Miss Broadus was presented to the School on this occasion by the Woman's Missionary Union of Kentucky and the family of Miss Broadus. The presentation was made by Miss Mary Nell Lyne, at that time executive secretary of Woman's Missionary Union of Kentucky.

Mrs. A. T. Robertson was the principal speaker, using as her subject, "Seeketh Not Her Own," as she gave a sketch of the life of Eliza S. Broadus.

Merging of the Two Boards

After eight years of inspiring leadership as president of Woman's Missionary Union, Mrs. W. J. Cox resigned in 1933 because of the serious illness of her husband. Mrs. F. W. Armstrong, president of the Missouri Woman's Missionary Union, was elected to fill the office.

She had been active in state and Southwide Woman's Missionary Union work for ten years. Her attractive physical appearance and personality had marked her early in this period as a forceful influence not only in Woman's Missionary Union but in the whole range of denominational work. In 1927 she was the first woman elected to membership on the Executive Committee of the Southern Baptist Convention.

She made no claims to being a good speaker. She frankly said to those closely associated with her that she felt that her contribution was in conference and committee work. Here she was a general of the first order. She had definite ideas of goals to be attained and procedures for attaining them, of ways to win approval of these goals and co-operation in working out the details.

Mrs. Armstrong had very definite ideas about the future of the School, and early in her term of office she began to work them out. The first problem to which she gave her attention was that of dual boards. This anomalous method of control was a natural result of the situation which existed in 1907 when Woman's Missionary Union took over what the Seminary and the Louisville women had already started, a home and a department of missionary training for women. In order to maintain and operate the home, a Board of Managers of representative Louisville Baptist women had been organized in 1904.

In those days travel was done sparingly, so in 1907 no one questioned the wisdom of retaining the local Board of Managers to supervise and direct the School at close range. Now, however, conditions were quite different, and Mrs. Armstrong set herself to correct the situation.

In connection with Founders' Day, 1936, she called a meeting of the General Board, composed of the local Board of Managers and the Board of Trustees. They were in session in October for three days and were led to make decisions of tremendous significance, one of which was the reorganization of the Board of Trustees.

On April 12, 1937, the local Board of Managers had its final meeting. In her final report as chairman of that Board, Mrs. Whayne reviewed again the situation that brought the Board into existence and the unselfish service rendered the struggling School in its early years by the Louisville women. There was no bitterness of spirit but rather an enveloping sadness as this "child of their love and prayers" finally slipped from the control of the original committee.

In New Orleans on May 10, 1937, the General Board had its final meeting. The amendment to the charter of Woman's Missionary Union Training School, adopted at the October, 1936, meeting of the Board and authorized for recording in the annual meeting minutes, reads in part as follows:

The affairs of the Corporation shall be conducted by a Board of Trustees consisting of the president, executive secretary and treasurer of the Woman's Missionary Union, one trustee from each state W.M.U. represented in the Southern Baptist Convention, three trustees at large and seven members, residents of Louisville, Kentucky. . . . All of the members of said Board of Trustees shall be elected annually by the Woman's Missionary Union.[6]

The Flood

If you say "flood" to a resident of Louisville of 1937 it would never occur to him to think of Noah's flood, because he had one of his own through which he floated not in an ark but in a rowboat, a canoe, or a motorboat through the streets of downtown Louisville. The school, located at that time in downtown Louisville, suffered the full force of the flood. Of all the difficulties of this difficult decade, perhaps the flood was the most disrupting.

Due to a warm January, which caused the rapid melting of the snow and ice in the upper Ohio River Valley, and unusually heavy rains, the river rose steadily, finally cresting eleven feet higher than its previous record in 1884. The central, western, and southern parts of the city of Louisville became one vast lake.

On Saturday, January 23, with the furnace room and kitchen in the basement flooded from water backing up through the drain pipes, it was evident that the School could no longer carry on. With the help of the local Board, the Seminary, and many Baptists of Louisville, the students were placed in homes in the Highland and Crescent Hill areas. After a day or two all of them were able to go to their homes.

Remaining at the School were eight patients in the infirmary, sick with colds and flu, and six resident members of the faculty and staff who chose to stay by to help care for the sick girls and the building. Fortunately, the weather was quite warm, so a few electric heaters and the big fireplace in the dining room on the main floor kept the group comfortable. The janitor, before conditions got too bad in the basement, brought up a supply of coal to keep the open fire going. Miss Mitchell, with the help of the two cooks and the janitor, transferred as much food as possible to the serving room adjoining the dining room, where a two-burner gas plate could be used for cooking. In such fashion the group felt confident that they could get along until the emergency was over.

This false assurance was rudely shattered, however, when by ten o'clock that Saturday night water was running freely in both Broadway and Preston Streets. With all records broken, there was no way of guessing what would happen. It was evident now that the building must be vacated.

By daylight next morning boats of every variety were running free taxi service on Broadway and other main streets. Soon a man appeared at the door saying the Lutheran minister across the street had sent him for the sick girls. They were wrapped up warmly and packed in the boat with the prayer that they would not catch their death of pneumonia.

Two Seminary students, John Hughston and M. O. Owens, who were helping with refugee work at Broadway Baptist Church two blocks down the street, came on call to help the janitor move everything movable from the first floor.

Well past noon the work was finished, and the group prepared to leave. The boys stood outside the front door and hailed the passing boatmen. Some were on emergency calls, others were on their way to the city hospital with patients. Finally, a motorboat came over to the door, and the man agreed to take the group out. On seeing the women and their bags, the boatman signaled a passing canoe and a rowboat. With their help the last of the Training School refugees were on their way to higher ground.

When the boat reached the end of Broadway at the foot of the hill, men were there standing in water waist deep, pulling boats in and lifting refugees out bodily. On dry land once more, they were put in cars to be taken to near-by churches for inoculation against typhoid and for assignment to homes open to refugees.

Nine days passed before it was possible to get back to see how the building fared. All in all, it was a desolate picture. The basement was still full of water. Kitchen tables, the old sideboard, a relic of the early days, boxes, and barrels were floating around; the marble hall and stairway were as muddy as the streets.

As soon as possible, Miss Mitchell began the tremendous task of cleaning the building. The water had to be pumped out of the basement, but before a pump could be secured most of it had drained out. The supplies, reduced to debris and rubbish, had to be carted up the steps by hand since the elevator was not running. The mud and slime had to be washed out and the whole place disinfected. The plumber spent several days reconditioning the furnace and restoring the plumbing and gas connections. The electricians repaired all wiring that had been under water. Gas service was restored on February 15 and electrical power the next day. With these necessary services restored, letters were sent to the students notifying them that classes would be resumed on Monday, February 22.

The Tie That Binds

One of the Shanghai newspapers, the *China Press*, dated February 2, 1937, carried the interesting story of a meeting in Shanghai of a group of leading businessmen to launch a campaign for $200,000 to aid flood refugees in America. One of this number, S. U. Zau, was not only a man of importance in civic affairs but a great Christian who had direct ties with the Woman's Missionary Union Training School through his wife, the former Miss Wu Ming Yung. It is easy to believe that this loyal graduate prompted her husband to start this gesture of friendship because her old school in Louisville was so directly affected by the flood. Nearer home, friends throughout the denomination, especially former students, sent in many personal offerings to help in the expensive repairs of the building.

The tie that binds Christians together around the world surmounts all barriers. The difficulties of the last decade faded into insignifiance in the renewed assurance that the School was still a beloved missionary project in the denomination.

5

Looking Toward the Future

Look not mournfully to the Past. It comes not again. Wisely improve the Present. It is thine.— HENRY W. LONGFELLOW

IT IS NECESSARY to turn back the pages of this story to 1936 in order to understand the beginning of this chapter of the School's history. Mrs. Armstrong called the Board of Trustees to Louisville in October of that year to put before them and the local Board her plans for the future of the School. Even though the effects of the depression were still evident and the denomination was laboriously paying its debts, she brought these plans fearlessly to the Board and led them to consider and approve them in their three-day conference.

Restoring Old Relationships

Mrs. Armstrong had already discussed the proposed changes with the Woman's Missionary Union Executive Committee and the state Woman's Missionary Union secretaries in Birmingham in January, and this group had authorized her to approach Dr. John R. Sampey, president of the Southern Baptist Seminary, regarding the developments that affected the Seminary. These plans were clearly explained in the "Findings of General Board of Woman's Missionary Union Training School, October 1–3, 1936."

In a long and detailed statement, the findings provided for the following changes: (1) to provide for the students to return to the Seminary for the majority of their classes in the

fall of 1937, if possible; (2) to provide bus transportation for
them, since there was no streetcar service to the Seminary;
(3) to appoint a committee, with power to act, to secure property near the Seminary; (4) to take adequate time to work
out plans for moving the School so that the downtown property
would not be sacrificed; (5) to continue the Good Will Center
and other city mission activities in case the School should
move to the neighborhood of the Seminary.[1]

Following the meetings of the Board of Trustees and the
Woman's Missionary Union Executive Committee in New
Orleans in May, 1937, Mrs. Armstrong issued a statement in
the religious press under the title, "Plans for the Woman's
Missionary Union Training School," in which she explained,
first of all, the merging of the two boards of the School. She
then reviewed the history of the beginnings, noting that "the
deciding factor in locating the School in Louisville was the advantage offered our students of studying with Seminary professors." She referred to the moving of the Seminary to "The
Beeches," which brought that old relationship to an end. She
said:

The Board, in its effort to carry out the wishes of the constituency
many of whom feel that the future progress of the school will be
promoted by the return to the relationship with the Seminary that
existed in the early years of the school, has found that such change
is not immediately possible but must await certain physical adjustments and sufficient increase in the faculty of the Seminary to
assure reduction in size of larger classes. Knowing that these problems require time and conference the Board has asked the Seminary faculty to arrange for the teaching of classes in Bible in our
school even as they have taken care of other courses that are du-
plicated. The Board keenly regrets that this change in policy makes
necessary the severing of the happy relation with Dr. McGinty.
The Board and the entire constituency of W.M.U. wishes him success in the challenging new task upon which he now enters.[2]

Before this statement was issued Dr. McGinty had already
been elected to the faculty of Bessie Tift College in Georgia,

131

could be taken for a simple Sunday evening meal in the dining room with leisurely fellowship as table groups talked of field work experiences and church services.

On Friday, April 8, 1938, news went out from Columbus, Georgia, that the eventide had fallen for Mrs. McLure. She had been ill for several months, so death was a happy release for her. The following Sunday she was laid to rest in Evergreen Cemetery, Chester, South Carolina, beside her beloved husband, Thomas E. McLure, and her son, Captain John Thomas McLure.

Mrs. McLure was born at "Mount Ida," the Reynolds colonial homestead in Talladega County, Alabama, April 25, 1862. Her father, Walker Reynolds, had bought the land from the Indians. He selected a site at the top of a rolling hill and there supervised the building of the colonial residence, an impressive mansion in a remarkably beautiful setting. Its natural loveliness was enhanced by boxwood hedges and gardens of rare flowers. To see "Mount Ida" is to know that Mr. and Mrs. Reynolds loved the beautiful. Mrs. McLure's mother was the daughter of a pioneer Baptist preacher, Oliver Welch, who came to Alabama from Virginia.

In this home of Christian culture, plenty, and privilege, Maud Reynolds, the youngest in a family of six children, developed into beautiful young womanhood. When only eight years of age she became a Christian and united with the Baptist church in the community where her grandfather was pastor and the other members of her family were active workers. Since public schools were few and far removed, as a child she was taught in the home by private instructors. When she was older she went to the school in Talladega, ten miles away. Later she entered Judson College at Marion, Alabama, and finally she attended a finishing school for young women in Baltimore, Maryland.

In Baltimore one of her best friends was Bessie McLure of Chester, South Carolina. When Maud visited the McLure

134

home, she met the young son, Thomas E. McLure. He was at once attracted to this charming Alabama girl and began to make regular visits to her beautiful home. According to the custom of the day, the courtship was unhurried. They were married at "Mount Ida" on January 20, 1886.

The young lawyer was already established in Chester, and there they made their home. After two years a baby boy came to gladden their lives. When the baby was but a year old, the young father died suddenly of a dental infection. Mrs. McLure wanted her son to grow up in the atmosphere of his father's native state, so she continued to live in Chester until 1895.

At that time, circumstances led her to launch out on a musical career, and she went to Columbus, Georgia, and established herself as a music teacher. In 1903 she accepted a position as voice teacher at Cox College in College Park, an Atlanta suburb. At the same time, her son entered the Georgia Military Academy, also located in College Park. It was an ideal arrangement for both of them.

Mrs. McLure had been in this work for four years when the insistent call came to her to go into a new and untried field. After prayerful consideration, she yielded to the call of God and went forth on her venture of faith. The proposed school was pioneer work for Southern Baptist women, and it would probably stand or fall according to the woman who would set its standards and draft its policies. In Mrs. McLure was found a woman equal to the task. Surely her life was divinely timed.

After all these years it is still difficult to evaluate adequately Mrs. McLure's unique contribution to the School. She gave to the School an indefinable atmosphere of Christian culture, an appreciation of the practical skills in missionary service, and a sane expression of personal religion. In the curriculum she sought from the beginning to keep balance between theoretical and practical courses. She emphasized the importance of the field work because she knew how easy it is for students in a deeply religious atmosphere to live apart from the world in their ivory towers. She was a strict disciplinarian in the finest sense of the word. She would not accept shoddy work. She had high standards for the School and for its students, and she was deeply hurt when they failed to measure up.

Dr. A. T. Robertson of the Seminary used to say he was called to "take the starch out of" ministerial students. That is a necessary but often thankless task. Young women, even those preparing to be missionaries, often need that same ministry. Many of Mrs. McLure's students lived to thank her for all that she did for them, even though it was painful at the time.

By nature and training she was richly endowed for her life work. She had poise, charm, dignity, tact, practical common sense, a keen sense of humor, and a rich personal religious life. She was a delightful conversationalist and a gracious hostess. It is a great thing for the kingdom of God when a woman of her ability and unusual gifts devotes herself to Christian service. She could have been a leader in many areas of life, but somewhere in her youth she heard the call of Jesus, and henceforth her powers were dedicated to the service of her Lord.

Mrs. McLure's death in 1938 marked the passing of the last of the five founders. Miss Heck died in 1915, Miss Broadus in 1931, Mrs. Eager and Mrs. Woody in 1933. What a remarkable group of women they were, and what a heritage they left not only to the School they loved and served but to the cause of missions in their day and ours!

Anniversary Year

The year 1938 marked the fiftieth anniversary of the Woman's Missionary Union. In deference to the Union, the Southern Baptist Convention voted to meet in Richmond, Virginia, so that the Golden Jubilee might be observed in the city where the organization had its birth in 1888.

The Training School was also having an anniversary as it

turned back the pages of its history to 1918, when the first commencement was held in the new building at Preston and Broadway. On that occasion a daring break with custom in Kentucky was made by having a woman deliver the commencement address. The speaker was Mrs. W. C. James, the president of Woman's Missionary Union. On the twentieth anniversary of that historic occasion Mrs. James again was the featured speaker.

In the program and the financial plans for the Golden Jubilee in Richmond, the Training School had a prominent place. In fact, the special Golden Jubilee project was an initial gift of $50,000 toward a new building for the School. The Tuesday afternoon program was given over to the presentation of the School and the report of the Golden Jubilee Committee, of which Mrs. George McWilliams was chairman.

At the beginning of the afternoon session a great host of alumnae joined with students in marching into the auditorium singing the traditional processional, "Take the Light." Seated on the platform, they provided an atmosphere for Mrs. McWilliams' report. She began with the statement:

. . . The special gift of $50,000 for a new, a better, a larger Training School is a special Golden Jubilee project and will go down in history as such. It is our "long thought . . . for the years" and the Training School alumnae seated on the platform represent the "dedication of our future" which must always be the important part of any anniversary. . . . Many things have transpired within the last decade that, in the judgment of the very great majority of our people, make the removal and rebuilding of the Training School a wise plan for the finest future development of the school.[3]

Following Mrs. McWilliams' report, the report of the Training School was given by the principal. The discussion included the story of the adoption of the School by Woman's Missionary Union in Richmond in 1907 by Mrs. J. B. Boatright, of South Carolina. The early struggles of the School were described by Miss Emma Leachman. The following Seminary professors who repeated their classes in the Training School were introduced: Dr. F. M. Powell, Dr. J. McKee Adams, Dr. H. W. Tribble, Dr. W. H. Davis, Dr. Kyle Yates, and Dr. W. O. Carver. From the special Training School faculty Miss Claudia Edwards, instructor in music, and Miss Wanda Lynch, director of the Good Will Center, were presented. The School's featured program was concluded with an address by Dr. Carver on "What the Future of the Training School May Be."

The Memorial Service concluding the afternoon program was conducted by Mrs. Ryland Knight, a former Training School student and a member of its Board of Trustees. Miss Littlejohn paid a tribute to Mrs. Maud R. McLure, who had passed away just one month before the Golden Jubilee meeting.

Building Plans and Progress

The Golden Jubilee gift for the new building went far beyond the goal of $50,000. At the next annual meeting the treasurer, Mrs. W. J. Cox, reported a total of $72,288.14.

The special committee appointed by Mrs. Armstrong to secure property in the neighborhood of the Seminary lost no time in carrying out its assignment. By August, 1937, Woman's Missionary Union had the deed to a beautiful tract of land containing seven and one-fourth acres adjacent to the Seminary campus on Lexington Road. The price paid was $27,500, a reasonable figure considering that the location is in one of the best and most rapidly growing residential sections of the city of Louisville.

At the annual meeting of the Board of Trustees in February, 1939, the decision was made to launch a campaign to raise an additional $100,000 during the next Convention year. At the annual session of Woman's Missionary Union in Oklahoma City the following May, the campaign was launched and the states agreed in their usual fine spirit to do their part in the joint undertaking. The treasurer was authorized to draw upon the Endowment and Enlargement Fund, if necessary, for the building project, with the understanding that upon the sale of the downtown property the said fund would be reimbursed.

The Building Committee included the following members: Mrs. F. W. Armstrong, Miss Kathleen Mallory, Mrs. W. J. Cox, and Miss Carrie U. Littlejohn for the Union; Mrs. J. C. Hering, Mrs. John R. Sampey, Mrs. Frank E. Short, and Mrs. E. M. Nuckols from the Board of Trustees; Mrs. J. Clyde Turner and Miss Juliette Mather from the Woman's Missionary Union Executive Committee; Miss Mary Nelle Lyne and Miss Louise Smith from the Alumnae Association.

This committee began its search for the architect promptly. Well in advance of the annual session of Woman's Missionary Union in May, 1939, the Louisville firm of Nevin, Morgan and Kolbrook had been selected and their first sketches studied. This well-known firm specialized in the Georgian style of architecture, so well suited to that section of the city. They assured the committee that the building would be planned in harmony with the Seminary buildings but distinctive in design. Their finished work beautifully fulfilled that pledge.

As the campaign for funds got under way, the $100,000 goal was named the Maud R. McLure Memorial. At the Woman's Missionary Union Executive Meeting in January, 1940, it was voted to place Mrs. McLure's portrait in the heart of the house with a plaque bearing this sentiment, ". . . To this building the W.M.U. of the South gave $100,000 as a memorial to Mrs. Maud Reynolds McLure, the first principal of the W.M.U. Training School." [4]

The financial goal was not reached in one year as planned, but by February, 1941, the treasurer reported to the Board of Trustees that the memorial to Mrs. McLure had been crowned with success. By May, 1941, she reported a total of $109,302.33. When the contributions were all in, the grand total was $111,-000.

It is to the everlasting credit of Woman's Missionary Union

that this large gift was raised in an extra effort while it was helping generously in another extra, the denominational debt-paying campaign. At the same time, regular gifts through the Cooperative Program and special offerings to home and foreign missions in March and December were increasing steadily each year.

All of this was done in an atmosphere of depression not far in the background, and of war inevitably closing in on the nation. Credit is due to the Union, also, for the fine spirit of co-operation that marked all its efforts. Where the Training School has been concerned, the women have always given joyously and generously, as to a well-beloved child. There was no holding back.

For daring to launch another money-raising campaign at such an inopportune time top honors should go to Mrs. Armstrong for her generalship. From the time she became president in 1933, she took this development of the School as her special project. By 1936 she was ready to initiate her plan. She worked out every detail and had the ability not only to interest her constituency in the idea but also to inspire them with enthusiasm in raising the money in spite of untoward conditions.

Special credit also is due Miss Kathleen Mallory for the success of the campaign. Personally, she opposed moving the School. Sentiment may have influenced her to some degree in her thinking. She belonged to the group who had put love, as well as money, into the beloved House Beautiful at 334 East Broadway. She could never be persuaded to go into the building after the School moved in 1941.

But she was moved not by sentiment alone—rather by the feeling that this was no time to launch another campaign for funds in view of conditions in the denomination and the world. Being remarkably democratic, however, when the project was approved by the Board of Trustees, the Woman's Missionary Union Executive Committee, and finally, the Union in annual session, she submerged her personal feelings and threw herself heartily into the campaign.

The Library

Attempts had been made through the years to develop an adequate library, but not until 1938 was the administration authorized to secure a trained librarian. Miss Mary Pratt, an employee of the Louisville Public Library and a member of the local Board for many years, had done some cataloging at the School and instructed two members of the faculty who worked at it in their spare time. Except for the cataloging, the library had been cared for by students.

In September, 1938, the School had the good fortune to secure the services of Miss Georgie Fancher, of Mississippi, to take over the library. It took her years to get the books properly cataloged while meeting current needs, but the present library is a monument to her patience, accuracy, and constructive work.

Magnifying Missionary Education

After eleven years of constructive work as teacher of missionary education, Miss Elsie Ragsdale resigned in 1939 to become dean of women in a college in South Carolina. As she left the school, the Board of Trustees expressed appreciation for the contribution which she had made to Woman's Missionary Union leadership.

At the annual meeting in 1939 the Board took the following action:

Careful consideration was given to the curriculum in general and to its Missionary Education Course in particular. Since the school is a missionary training school it was deemed desirable to magnify greatly the missions courses. It was therefore decided to establish the Department of Missions with Dr. W. O. Carver as head professor and the teacher of Missionary Education as assistant. By unanimous vote Miss Mary Christian of Georgia was elected as the

141

assistant. Discussion brought out the fact that, since Missionary Education is the emphasis upon W.M.U. ideals and methods, its teaching would be greatly strengthened through the instructors having wide and varied contact with the W.M.U. constituency, which in turn would be even more closely bound to the School's every interest. Accordingly by action of the W.M.U. Executive Committee it was determined that Miss Christian as a W.M.U. representative shall travel as extensively as her duties at the School will justify.[5]

Miss Christian came into her work of teaching with an excellent background as Young People's secretary in Arkansas and Georgia and executive secretary of the Woman's Missionary Union of Georgia.

Because of her exceptional contribution as a field worker, the Woman's Missionary Union Executive Committee in 1941 asked the Board of Trustees to release her for much-needed general field work.

The Good Will Center Sold

In August, 1940, the Good Will Center was sold to the Presbyterian Colored Mission. For twenty-eight years the Center had served one of the neediest sections of the city. At the same time, it had given valuable training to hundreds of students in the area of good will center work and city missions. During the last few years, however, there had been a decided shift in population. The Italian and Jewish people had gradually moved to better residential sections as they became more prosperous. As they had moved out, Negroes had moved in. The School was now faced with a real problem. If the Center should be converted to a Negro center, would it continue to be as valuable as a clinic for students?

In the nature of things very few of the students would work with Negroes after they left school. Furthermore, the Presbyterian Colored Mission directed by Dr. John Little had for many years been working with Negroes in that section. The School had co-operated by sending to that mission a group of student workers every year. It was unthinkable that the School would now compete with Dr. Little.

Fortunately, providential circumstances solved the dilemma. The flood in 1937 left the building used by the Presbyterian Colored Mission in bad condition. It hardly seemed worth while to try to repair it, so the people who attended it had been transferred to another mission several blocks away. They had never been happy, however, and were constantly urging Dr. Little to reopen a mission in their neighborhood. He was impressed to approach the School about the matter, and the sale was consummated in a few weeks. Because it was to continue to be used as a Christian center, the Good Will Center building was sold for $16,000.

Due to unsettled social and economic conditions in Louisville at that time and also to the lack of time on the part of the Board and the faculty to study so important a matter, it was decided to postpone any plans for opening new work until after the School was settled in its new location. The money received from the sale of the property was invested for future good will center development.

Breaking Ground

It was March 20, 1940, a clear, cold, windy afternoon, the sort of day that ushers in spring in Kentucky. The Board of Trustees was in session. They had postponed their meeting from the usual February date so that they might participate in this great occasion—breaking ground for the new building.

A crowd had assembled well in advance of the hour for the ceremony—Training School students by chartered buses; faculty members, members of the Board of Trustees, and Louisville friends by cars; Seminary students hurrying from class and library across the way; little boys running ahead and climbing the trees to see it all well done. The crowd filled the level area where the building would stand and spilled over on the hillside toward the Seminary.

143

Mrs. Armstrong, radiantly happy, presided. Her dream was becoming a reality! The Training School chorus, directed by Miss Edwards, and the Seminary chorus, directed by Professor Inman Johnson, expressed praise and reverence in beautiful anthems, "Hear as we sing before Thy throne, Alleluia, Alleluia," and "Holy, Holy, Holy, God, Almighty Lord."

Dr. Carver had been asked to be the speaker, and who else could be "the voice for all whose interest seeks expression today"? He reminded his hearers that the Training School was not buildings or material equipment but a spirit that lived in the "temporary housings in the first years, that sanctified the present House Beautiful in which it grew and lived, and that will be the life and the glory of the statelier mansions it shall find on this expansive range of lovely landscape." And then Dr. Carver further enlarged his idea of the School as a spirit —a spirit of praise, of faith, of service, of hope, of love.

After the inspiring music and stirring address came the ground breaking. There was the new spade, gilded for the occasion, the gift of Dr. John Little of the Presbyterian Mission. And turning the first spade of earth was Mrs. Armstrong. This was her hour! Woman's Missionary Union was her very life, and the School was the Union's most beloved project. She had been concerned about its future, and that future, she was convinced, could be assured by the return to the old relationship. This for which she had dreamed and planned had been brought to pass.

Miss Mallory, representing Woman's Missionary Union, whose gifts of money and love undergirded the project, followed Mrs. Armstrong. Miss Fannie Moses, the last of the original Board, turned a spade for the founders; Miss Leachman for the "Big Four" of 1904; Dr. C. S. Gardner for the first faculty; Dr. Sampey for the present faculty; Miss Littlejohn for the School; Miss Ruth Provence for the Alumnae Association; Miss Elsie Renfroe for the student body; the members of the Board of Trustees for their respective states.

A hush fell over the group as the honored president of the Seminary, Dr. Sampey, the well-beloved teacher of Training School students from 1907 to 1926, led in the prayer of dedication—of the soil on which they stood, of the building that would arise, of the students who would come to learn in order that they might go and tell. At the end of the prayer the Training School chorus sang quietly the benediction, "The Lord bless thee and keep thee."

Mrs. Ryland Knight, in her charming account of this program, said in her closing paragraph:

The smile of God was reflected in the faces of those who turned away from the holy hour to go our several ways to try to interpret to the world the full meaning of this new day in Training School history. No words could picture the emotions of our hearts . . . no picture could bring to you the thrill of the beauty of the setting . . . nor can time erase from our memory the consciousness of the fact that here again we raise our Ebenezer.[6]

Laying the Cornerstone

The contract for the new building had been given to the F. W. Owens Construction Company. Mr. Owens was a Baptist, a tithing layman, and a man with a fine reputation as a builder. He began work promptly on April 1, and progress during the summer was uninterrupted.

Founders' Day, October 2, 1940, was chosen as the day for laying the cornerstone. Providence smiled on this outdoor ceremony with a clear sky, warm sunshine, and leaves beginning to put on their royal colors. Training School and Seminary students, faculty and Board members, Louisville and out-of-town friends came again in large numbers to share in this historic service. Mrs. Armstrong presided, communicating her vivid interest and enthusiasm to her audience. Dr. Carver in the invocation prayed that to this building might be transferred the spirit of sacrifice and service which had marked the School since its beginning in 1907.

145

Miss Juliette Mather, Young People's secretary of Woman's Missionary Union, representing the alumnae, made the first address. Dr. John R. Sampey, president of the Seminary, followed her with a stirring address on the words used on the cornerstone at the downtown building, "Our daughters . . . as cornerstones hewn after the fashion of a palace."

The Training School chorus sang a hymn, "O Thou Thrice Happy, Happy Place," which had been sung at the cornerstone-laying service in April, 1917. Then the articles of historic interest were placed in a copper box by the principal as they were brought to her by representatives of many groups. The box was sealed by one of the workmen and placed in its niche in the cornerstone. The closing prayer was led by Miss Mallory and the "Golden Jubilee Benediction," words and music by Rose Goodwin Pool, was sung by the Young People's secretaries who had come to Louisville for this service.

At the conclusion of the program, students, faculty, and out-of-town visitors were entertained at a tea at the home of Mrs. A. T. Robertson.

Founders' Day, 1940

This Founders' Day was also made memorable by the presence of the first four students, the "Big Four," who lived in the first home provided by Louisville women in 1904. It was an unusual providence that after thirty-seven years these four could be together for their first reunion and, at the same time, participate in two such significant services in the life of the School in which they played such a vital part at its beginning. Miss Leachman, the dynamic city missionary who had shared the little home with them, was at the service to lead in prayer. A passage of Scripture was read by Mrs. G. E. Henderson, of Tennessee, (Clemmie Ford), an active worker in her church and community. Mrs. J. W. Shepard, of Louisiana, (Rena Groover), for many years a missionary to Brazil, talked of "The Great Adventure" that brought them together in Louisville. Mrs. E. J. Comerford, of Texas, (Ella Jeter) told how the Training School began. She was a missionary in China for many years, but circumstances had brought her back to Texas where she was teaching in the public schools. Miss Alice Huey, of Alabama, chose to talk about her work in China, where she had served since her student days.

Final Plans for the New Building

During the annual session of the Board of Trustees in Louisville in February, 1941, final plans were made for the move to the new building. Ways of securing the necessary new equipment and furnishings were considered. A committee was appointed to begin a study of Louisville in order to find the best location for a good will center. It was decided to perpetuate in the new building the names of the five founders.

It was the wish of all concerned that the chapel would continue the memorial to Miss Heck. Mrs. McLure would be memorialized through the Union's gift of $111,000. East, central, and west halls in the dormitory would bear the names Broadus, Eager, and Woody. A series of dedications was planned for the different groups directly interested in the School. A homecoming for former students was scheduled for September just before the opening of the session.

One afternoon, during the Board's meeting, was given over to a tour of the new building, and even in its half-finished state it gave evidence of the beauty that was promised. There was no waiting for the outside beauty. Every window commanded a magnificent view.

Commencement, 1941

The enrolment had been steadily growing during the last few years as economic conditions improved and the denomination paid its way out from under the burden of debt. During this last year in the downtown building 105 boarding and 85 day students had enrolled.

On May 7 and 8 the final commencement services were held at the location that had been so well known for thirty-four years, 334 East Broadway. Miss Hannah Reynolds, niece of Mrs. McLure and former teacher of missionary education in the School, and at that time president of the Alumnae Association, was the speaker for the vesper service.

The final service in the original Heck Memorial Chapel on Thursday evening, May 8, was inspiring. Dr. W. O. Carver, the one member of the faculty who had been connected with the School continuously since its beginning in 1904, was the speaker. His subject was "The Gift of Christ to Women and His Gift of Women to the World."

Approximately 2300 young women had studied in the School up to that time and had come under his influence. He had seen them on their mission fields in South America, Japan, and China. He had observed them in their work on home mission fields and in large and small churches. They had a growing appreciation of him as a friend and a teacher as experience helped them to understand his profound ideas.

In the closing moments of his address "he pointed out the difficulties which women have had in entering with freedom the fields of service for which they were endowed by the spirit of God. . . . He also pointed out that it was in the cause of missions that women found first their opportunities and demonstrated their ability." [7]

Dr. John R. Sampey pronounced the benediction. Through his tender words the audience was made to feel that they were parting with an old friend who had served her day and generation well and was now graciously giving place to another.

Disposition of the Old Building

Shortly after the session closed in early May, a fifty-year lease was signed by which Radio Station WAVE took over the downtown building for its offices, studios, and auditorium.

The terms of the lease provided for a rental of $3,000 the first year, $5,000 per annum for the next two years, and $7,500 per annum for the next seven years. The lessee took an option to purchase the property within the first ten years for the sum of $160,000.

If the corporation did not purchase the property within the ten-year period, the rental and purchase price would increase decidedly thereafter. Toward the end of the tenth year the corporation bought the property at the price agreed upon in the 1941 lease. According to the plan adopted during the campaign for building funds, the building was considered an investment of endowment funds, and consequently the money realized from the sale was added to the endowment.

Moving Day

If there is some special reward for one who quietly and without complaint does the hard physical work in a religious institution with no thought of credit or recognition, Miss Mary Mitchell, house director and dietitian at the school for nineteen years, doubtless will receive a triple award and a "master of moving" degree. Three times in its history the School has moved, and each time Miss Mitchell has happened to inherit the hard job. She learned from the first two moves many valuable lessons which helped her to organize the packing for her third move in a methodical way.

After commencement was over and the students were out of the way, the final packing began in good earnest. One special job during that last month was the cleaning and packing of the books in the library. The cooks were used for this service, and one of them in particular got bored with the job. As she sat and dusted one book after another, she asked Miss Mitchell, "Does anybody ever read these books?"

Miss Mitchell explained to her that the books were used by the students in their class work. As the cook walked through the hall, however, she passed a teacher's room where books

149

were being sorted, dusted, and packed, and in passing she heard the teacher say, "I'm going to throw away some of these books. I haven't seen inside many of them for years."

The cook hurried back to the library and in triumph announced to Miss Mitchell, "Uh huh! I told you so! I just heard one of the teachers say she ain't seen inside some of her books for years. You can't fool me! I know nobody ain't ever gonna read all these books!"

Packing went steadily forward until June 10 when the actual moving began. On that day the giant vans began loading at the Preston Street door and methodically transferred the equipment and furnishings to the new building. Members of the faculty and staff who were needed to help with the tremendous undertaking had chosen to transfer their personal things and take up residence in their new quarters on Friday, the thirteenth. It would be easier to get through the week end in the new building than to exist in the desolate place that had been stripped of its beauty and personality.

Miss Mitchell announced at lunch on moving day that a makeshift supper would be served from scraps in the refrigerator. In the late afternoon the familiar old bell which had called to classes, to chapel, and to meals for twenty-four years sounded for the last time. The weary movers found their way to the dining room. During the afternoon the tables, the chairs, the piano, and the portrait of Miss Evie Brown had been moved out. One table and a few chairs were left.

It was a dreary outlook for the last meal in a house where there had been the kind of gracious living that made it a home. Stripped of everything but memories—of the farewell banquet for Mrs. McLure; the beautiful luncheon for Miss Broadus; a Christmas dinner with Dr. and Mrs. Robertson as the special guests, when the unpredictable "Dr. Bob" left the guest table and went to a window to see the fire trucks pass; a luncheon marking the wedding anniversary of Dr. and Mrs. Eager; Dr. Mullins telling one of his inimitable stories during a

Christmas dinner while fragile Mrs. Mullins sat and ate crackers and milk; beautifully dressed young women moving graciously among their guests at their many well-planned parties —this last meal itself became a poignant memory. When it was over, the little group went silently down the long hall, their steps a hollow echo through the empty building, picked up their baggage, and went out into Preston Street, closing the door on a phase of life that already seemed far removed in time. It was early twilight. A day was closing in Louisville. A day had closed in the history of the Woman's Missionary Union Training School.

Mrs. W. O. Carver, whose facile pen had helped to raise the money to build this home for the School, expressed for all who loved it a tender farewell in the following poetic lines:

> Dear House Beautiful,
> For four and twenty years
> We've loved you, admired you, adored you.
>
> We love your spacious halls,
> Parlors, classrooms, chapel and all
> The nooks and corners where we've found happiness,
> Calmness for our fears—and sometimes tears.
>
> We stand enraptured before your marble stairway,
> Your stained glass window
> That gleams and glows
> With every ray of sun that seeks and finds it.
>
> To thousands have you been a haven,
> A foretaste of eternal Heaven.
> And now we are to say good-bye to you—
>
> Not with tears we go,
> But with hearts aglow—
> Thrilled with gratitude for what you've been to us.
>
> To the new House Beautiful,
> We would take with us your spirit of friendliness,

Yet leave a portion to any
Who in future years
Shall dwell within your walls.

Dear, dear House Beautiful, good-bye.
God bless us in the going,
God bless you in the staying.

6

The New Day

This day only is ours: we are dead to yesterday,
and not born to to-morrow.—JEREMY TAYLOR

AN IMPORTANT FACTOR in the moving of a school is to carry over into the new home the love and loyalty of the old students. A homecoming, therefore, was planned for the alumnae for the week before the session opened in September, 1941. About 175 responded, representing most of the classes from 1908 to 1941 and practically every state of the Convention.

The building, though different in design in every particular from the downtown building, gave the old girls a sense of being at home as they saw the familiar portraits of Dr. Frost, the founders, Miss Evie Brown, and Henrietta Hall Shuck; as they listened to the chimes of the clock in the lobby, and as they enjoyed favorite dishes on Training School menus.

There were other planned activities to make them feel at home, such as assigned housework as in student days; stunt night in the recreation room, when classes dramatized the amusing incidents of their student generation; chapel on two mornings, led by the beloved teachers, Dr. Sampey and Dr. Carver; classes with Dr. Tribble, Dr. Adams, and Dr. Dobbins; discussion groups with Dr. Goerner and Dr. Weatherspoon.

The New Building Dedicated

The highlight of the crowded homecoming was the first of a series of dedications. The dramatic program based on Mrs.

McLure's "Lasting Foundations," written for the downtown building, was arranged by Miss Juliette Mather. Miss Hannah Reynolds, the president of the Alumnae Association, presided at this service. The Alma Mater hymn, written especially for the dedication by Rose Goodwin Pool, was sung for the first time. The beautiful anthem "Dedication," also composed by Mrs. Pool, was sung by a group of former students under Mrs. Pool's direction. These special numbers were featured at each of the succeeding dedicatory services.

At a business session the alumnae voted to buy a station wagon to be used in transporting students to their field work assignments. They also decided to start a fund toward the purchase of an organ for the chapel.

The first session in the new building opened September 16, 1941. During the year one hundred boarding and ninety day students enrolled. The fact that the student body was smaller than the year before was probably due to the disturbed conditions caused by the inevitable approach of war.

The one new member of the faculty that year was Miss Mary Nelle Lyne, who had been elected as teacher of missionary education to succeed Miss Mary Christian.

Miss Lyne's training and experience gave her a rich background for this work. She had been appointed in 1917 by the Foreign Mission Board for educational work in China, where she served for ten years as principal of the Cantonese Girls' School in Shanghai. In 1927 the school was closed because of war conditions, and Miss Lyne came home. Back in this country she served as Woman's Missionary Union secretary in Alabama, and later in her own state, Kentucky. From the latter position she came to her work at the Training School.

The formal opening exercises of the session provided the occasion for the second dedication. In a brief ceremony faculty and students accepted the building as God's gift and recognized their obligation to do better work in preparation and teaching.

On Founders' Day, October 2, 1941, the formal dedication of the building took place with Mrs. Armstrong making the address on the subject, "Lighted to Lighten." Greetings were brought by Mr. J. H. Anderson, chairman of the Seminary's Board of Trustees; Dr. Charles E. Maddry, secretary of the Foreign Mission Board; Dr. T. L. Holcomb, secretary of the Sunday School Board; and Mrs. J. H. Anderson, former principal of the School. Dr. Sampey led in the dedicatory prayer, and Dr. Carver led in the opening and closing prayers.

With skill and understanding Mrs. Armstrong traced the rich heritage of the School from its very small beginning in 1904 under the guidance of the Seminary and the loving ministry of Louisville women down to the present. She paid tribute to the founders and to Dr. Mullins. She expressed gratitude to Dr. Sampey and Dr. Carver for their loyal support and constructive help. In the climax of her stirring address, she said:

Today it must be recognized that the signal blessings of God which have attended this entire project, the story of which reads like a modern miracle, carry an obligation of extraordinary weight. The administrators of this School, its faculty, its student body, its trustees and sustaining Woman's Missionary Union are summoned to a re-evaluation of its high purposes under God and to a reconsecration of self that its ideals may live and grow, its service be broadened to meet the tremendous appeal of world need. Today we are dedicating not alone a building. Its beauty of form and appointments, its adequacy to present needs would be but a mockery if the soul which it houses were not completely dedicated to God and to the ongoing of His Kingdom in the world.[1]

This was a high hour in Mrs. Armstrong's life. It was for this she had dreamed daringly, planned largely, worked untiringly since 1936. She loved Woman's Missionary Union as she loved her own life. She considered the School the Union's most valuable asset. Now that she was certain its future was assured, she felt that the Union was thereby strengthened and its missionary purpose multiplied, for "the best teaching in the best environment seemed to its sponsors the best provision for its continued service to a needy world." [2]

In the evening a formal dinner brought the day to a close. The architects, contractor, faculty members and their wives, and the local members of the Board of Trustees and their husbands were the honored guests. The program, built on the theme "Dreamers of Dreams," featured Mrs. J. B. Weatherspoon in a tribute to the women who, under the leadership of Mrs. Armstrong, had worked to make the new building possible. In turn, Mrs. Armstrong paid tribute to the men whose "dreams grow holy put into action," especially recognizing the architects and the contractor.

Never was a building so completely dedicated as the new building of the Woman's Missionary Union Training School. The annual meeting of the Board of trustees was held at the School in late February, 1942, and the fourth and final dedication took place in the Heck Memorial Chapel on the evening of February 25.

The program, presided over by Mrs. Armstrong, included addresses by Dr. Annie D. Denmark, president of Anderson College, and Miss Kathleen Mallory, executive secretary of Woman's Missionary Union. In the service of dedication responses were made by Miss Nancy Cooper for the student body, Miss Littlejohn for the faculty, and Mrs. Ryland Knight for the Board of Trustees. The special music provided by Miss Edwards and the School's chorus included the hymn, "We Would Be Building," as well as the special dedication numbers. Mrs. W. J. Cox led in the closing prayer.

Mrs. Armstrong had announced at the dedication on October 2 that every bill had been paid and the building, therefore, was being dedicated free of debt. The money borrowed from the Endowment and Enlargement Fund ($145,700) was now considered invested in the building at Preston and Broadway.

The report of Mrs. W. J. Cox, treasurer of Woman's Missionary Union, at the annual session of the Union in May, 1942, carried the following information: income for building from all sources $353,729.27; expenditures: the building, $301,143.28; grading, drives, terrace, landscaping, initial planting, $29,-026.15; surety bond, insurance, miscellaneous, $3,573.69; architects, $19,273.73; total, $353,016.85; cash balance building fund, $712.42.

Getting Started in the New Day

Mrs. Armstrong faced a keen disappointment in the plans for classes in the new location. The administration at the Seminary did not agree in 1941 for Training School students to return to Seminary classrooms. They could continue to attend seminars and elective courses where the enrolment was relatively small, as they had done for several years, but the corridors and large classrooms where Bible classes met were not planned for such a sudden influx of women students. Mrs. Armstrong, though disappointed, was not dismayed. She accepted the ultimatum for the present with the confidence that the old relationship could be fully restored in time.

The activities in the field work department had to be drastically curtailed because of the transportation problem, but even so, every student had some service project to which she reported at least once a week. The station wagon provided by the Alumnae Association and the School car took the students in groups for afternoon or evening field work assignments.

Full Coeducation Again

In 1942 Dr. Sampey retired as president of the Seminary but was retained on the faculty as president emeritus and lecturer in the Old Testament department. Dr. Ellis A. Fuller, pastor of the First Baptist Church of Atlanta, Georgia, succeeded him. Mrs. Armstrong sought an interview with Dr. Fuller well in advance of the opening of the session.

As a result of this and succeeding conferences, in which

Dr. Fuller and the Seminary faculty and Mrs. Armstrong and the Executive Committee of the School's Board of Trustees participated, a satisfactory arrangement was worked out whereby Training School students were admitted again to all Seminary classes. In return, the combined remuneration, amounting to $8,430, which was being paid to Seminary professors for their teaching at the Training School, was turned over to the Seminary. This arrangement enabled the Seminary to give all of its professors an equitable raise in salary.

The next year the annual contribution to the Seminary was raised to $15,000. The same amount was included in the School's budget each year through the 1952–1953 session. Since that time Carver students enrol directly in the Seminary for such classes as fit into their schedule of studies, and the School pays the usual matriculation fees required of all Seminary students. This has proved to be a more equitable plan for both schools.

The Pinch of War

In addition to the major heartaches and sacrifices demanded by war, the School suffered many inconveniences that affected its life and work. There was the problem of gas and tire rationing. In order to stay within the limited allotment the field work had to be drastically reduced again. It was necessary to eliminate the churches and centers farthest removed from the campus and concentrate on the centers that were easily accessible.

Another problem, which added to the dietitian's difficulties and affected the morale of the student body, was that of getting food in quantity, quality, and variety to provide well-balanced meals.

As the war went on it became increasingly difficult to get and keep servants. The problem had started during the first year in the new location because of transportation difficulties. The nearest bus service was three or four blocks across the back campus. The competition of war plant wages added to the problem, and often the result was no cooks.

One of those days was a certain Monday when Miss Mitchell and Mrs. Judy, her assistant, with the help of some students, prepared and served breakfast, lunch, and dinner so smoothly and so promptly that the majority of the group did not know of the emergency in the kitchen.

It so happened that on this particular evening the Cincinnati Symphony Orchestra was giving a concert in Louisville, and most of the faculty and staff members had tickets. Miss Mitchell and Mrs. Judy, in spite of their long, hard day, were dressed and ready to go at the appointed time. They probably needed a change of atmosphere!

The first number on the program was an exquisite composition for strings. The applause was an ovation. The teacher next to Miss Mitchell turned to her to remark on the beauty of the music. Miss Mitchell agreed as she continued to applaud and turned to Mrs. Judy with a remark. Mrs. Judy nodded assent and murmured a few words without ever hesitating in her applause. The teachers immediately behind them were convulsed with laughter. One of them leaned over and said to Miss Mitchell's companion, "Did you hear what they were saying while they applauded? Miss Mitchell asked Mrs. Judy if she had to make more gravy, and Mrs. Judy said that was the reason she was late getting into the dining room for dinner!"

The Passing Parade

To be connected with an institution is to realize that its small world is a series of changes. Personalities emerge and make their contributions, then move on in the passing parade to give place to others.

In 1943 two of the most beloved of Seminary and Training School professors, Dr. Sampey and Dr. Carver, retired from active service. Both of these distinguished teachers continued to lecture and supply in their respective departments as long as their health permitted. It was always a memorable experience to students when they could hear them either in class or in chapel.

At the commencement luncheon for the fifty-six members of the graduating class of 1943 these honored professors and their wives, together with Dr. and Mrs. Fuller, were the special guests.

Mrs. George J. Sutterlin, who had served on the faculty as speech teacher for twenty-four years, retired in 1942. Miss Anne Tennant, of Virginia, succeeded her. After two years Miss Tennant resigned to make her contribution to the war effort by taking up recreational work under the American Red Cross. Miss Miriam Robinson, of Georgia, succeeded Miss Tennant. She was one of the few graduates of the School equipped by training to do this important work.

Miss Mary Ellen Wooten, of Georgia, was elected to the position of field work supervisor in 1944. In addition to this major responsibility, Miss Wooten taught the classes in social work and personal evangelism. Two years later she was appointed by the Foreign Mission Board for educational work in Nigeria.

After five years as teacher of missionary education Miss Mary Nelle Lyne resigned in 1946 to work with Chinese people in California under the Home Mission Board. Miss Virginia Wingo, young people's secretary in Louisiana, succeeded Miss Lyne. In 1949 Miss Wingo was appointed by the Foreign Mission Board to the Armstrong Memorial Training School in Rome, Italy.

Miss Elaine Neeley was asked to take over the missionary education classes following Miss Wingo's resignation. In 1952, when there was an acute need for a financial secretary at the School, Miss Neeley was asked to shift to that position. Being capable in more than one field has its drawbacks!

While a graduate student and until her appointment by the Foreign Mission Board, Miss Martha Hairston, of Arkansas, was instructor in social work courses and director of field work. When she went to Brazil in 1951, Miss Kathryn Bigham, who had served as a missionary in Shanghai for one term, was secured to direct field work and develop a department of church social work. Since she could not continue her work in China, it seemed providential that she could use her advanced social work training and her missionary experience in helping to prepare students for missionary service at home and abroad.

The year 1948 marked the retirement of Miss Mary Mitchell, who had served the School with unusual devotion for nineteen years. Miss Claudia Edwards in a tribute to her expressed the sentiments of all her co-workers:

> As she went about her heavy duties, she always maintained that calmness and patience so characteristic of her. . . . To those of us who watched Miss Mitchell go through the war years, she is one of the wonders of the world. There was the constant problem of food and household supplies; there was the ever present permit from and report to the ration board; there was the daily fear of losing servants—a fear which materialized innumerable times. . . . We are happy to see her go to sunny California where she can live a quiet life. But will she? I doubt it! [3]

How fortunate the School has been to have had two such capable and loyal Kentucky women as Miss Warren and Miss Mitchell in its food and housekeeping departments for thirty-three of its fifty years. On the honor roll of those who have served with distinction in difficult positions, their names lead all the rest.

The year 1948 also marked the retirement of Miss Kathleen Mallory as executive secretary of Woman's Missionary Union. She had been elected to this office in 1912 when the School was suffering from growing pains, and through all the years of its development she had served its cause with devotion as a member of its Board of Trustees.

Miss Alma Hunt, of Virginia, succeeded Miss Mallory not

only in service to the Union but also to the Training School, the child of the Union. Her interest in its work has endeared her to the faculty, staff, and students alike.

This year, 1948, that brought so many changes to the School, also marked the passing of a title, that of principal. After much discussion over a long period of time, the Board of Trustees finally voted to call the head of the School its president.

The Death of Mrs. Armstrong

Death came suddenly to Mrs. F. W. Armstrong on May 13, 1945. She loved life and crowded it with worthy service. She was busy until two days before her death. She would not have spent her last days differently. Enforced inactivity would have been difficult for her.

Mrs. Armstrong was president of Woman's Missionary Union from 1933 until her death. By virtue of that office she was chairman of the Woman's Missionary Union Training School's Board of Trustees. No other president had ever taken such an active part in the School's life. She considered it the most valuable possession of the Union and tried to guide it into channels of greatest service to the Union and to the cause of missions. It was said of her that "the erection of the Woman's Missionary Union Training School, Louisville, Ky., stands as a monument in brick and stone, testifying to her vision, efficiency and tireless devotion to the cause of missions." [4]

Mrs. Armstrong also was a member of the Executive Committee of the Southern Baptist Convention from 1927 until her death in 1945. One of her last services to the Training School was through her work on that committee securing a full 1 per cent of the Cooperative Program funds for the School, beginning in 1945. Prior to that year the allotment had been only $\frac{8}{15}$ of 1 per cent.

Her last visit to the School was late in March, when she attended the Executive Committee meeting of the Board of Trustees. Miss Mallory in writing of that meeting said:

162

There she wisely guided in many decisions, among them being the purpose to ask Woman's Missionary Union to help largely in securing the $100,000.00 sorely needed by the Southern Baptist Theological Seminary in providing at least six new classrooms.[5]

Shortly after the present building was completed in 1941, the Board of Trustees named the beautiful terrace on the north side of the building the "Armstrong Terrace" in honor of Mrs. Armstrong's leadership in raising the money for the ambitious project of moving the School to its new location.

The New WMU President

Because of war restrictions on travel there was no annual meeting of Woman's Missionary Union in 1945. The Woman's Missionary Union Executive Committee in this emergency had the responsibility of meeting to elect a president. The committee met in Birmingham in July and elected Mrs. George R. Martin, who had served as the president of the Woman's Missionary Union of Virginia and vice-president of the Southern Union for seventeen years. She came into the new responsibility, therefore, with understanding of its purposes and problems.

From her first official visit to the School as chairman of the Board of Trustees, the faculty and staff found in Mrs. Martin a warm, sympathetic friend. The members of the Board were likewise delighted to find this first lady of the Union not only an expert and gracious presiding officer but also a very charming and human person to know.

Contribution to Seminary Classroom Building

While Mrs. Armstrong was attending the Executive Committee meeting of the Board of Trustees in March shortly before her death, the president of the Seminary discussed with her the possibility of getting help from Woman's Missionary Union for the new classroom wing to be added to Norton Hall. Because Mrs. Armstrong felt so deeply that the Training School's future depended on its continued close co-operation

163

with the Seminary, she was most sympathetic and agreed to bring the matter before the Woman's Missionary Union Executive Committee at its next meeting.

In order to get the matter immediately into the thinking of as many members of the Executive Committee as possible, she sent a message to the local members of the committee as they met early in April. She told of her recent visit to Louisville and of Dr. Fuller's request for help in building the new classroom wing at the Seminary. She then presented two recommendations from the Executive Committee of the Board of Trustees "that Woman's Missionary Union undertake to provide $50,000 of the estimated $100,000 needed; that the receipts accruing to the School from the proposed April Centennial Thank Offering be applied toward this objective." [6]

The minutes of the Woman's Missionary Union Executive Committee record that final action on the first of the two recommendations had to be taken by the full Woman's Missionary Union Executive Committee. Since the second recommendation called for immediate action, it was moved and carried "that any amount accruing to the Woman's Missionary Union Training School from the Centennial Thank Offering in April be applied toward this $50,000 goal." [7]

As a matter of unfinished business it was necessary to bring to the Woman's Missionary Union Executive Committee at its special meeting in July the request for the $50,000, and it was discussed from every angle. There were problems that Mrs. Armstrong apparently had not anticipated when she sent the recommendation to Birmingham in April. By this time there were two other seminaries in the Convention. The friends of these institutions made it very clear that Woman's Missionary Union could not aid in a building campaign for Southern Seminary without giving similar help to the other two. Finally, a solution to the difficult problem was reached by taking $50,000 from the Training School's reserve funds for the Seminary's building project.

Statistics and Standards

Beginning in 1943 the enrolment made a decided comeback. Recovering from the first shock of war and free from the debts that had shackled the denomination for several years, the mission boards began expanding their work. At the same time, other avenues of service were opened. The trend upward continued until 1947 when 135 boarding students were crowded into the dormitory. In 1948 there were seventy-eight members of the graduating class, the largest in the School's history.

As the enrolment increased the faculty and Board of Trustees were led to take another forward step in the entrance requirements. After 1945 no students with less than two years of college work were admitted except as special students.

Recognizing the maturity needed in missionary appointees and leadership in Christian service at home, a further step was taken that year by giving preference to applicants who had, in addition to four years in college, at least one year of experience in some kind of work.

The missionary emphasis and opportunities were again stirring students with old-time missionary zeal. The Training School has usually led the seminaries in percentage of former students serving with the Foreign Mission Board. In 1946 at the April meeting of the Board, sixteen of the forty-four missionaries appointed were products of the Training School.

In 1947 when the fortieth anniversary of the School was being observed without fanfare, it was found that 280 of the three thousand students who had enrolled had gone as foreign missionaries. Accurate records had not been kept on those going into home mission work.

In 1949, when a study was made of the graduates for the period 1943–1947, it was found that 32 per cent had gone into mission work, 7 per cent into Woman's Missionary Union work, 35 per cent into church work, 12 per cent into student work, 8 per cent into weekday religious education, 6 per cent into college teaching, 5 per cent into Sunday school and Training Union work, and 20 per cent to public school teaching and business positions. Since many of the graduates had held more than one position during the period, the total number of positions was larger than the number of persons polled.

Another check made in 1948 gave reason for pride in the School's part in the foreign missionary enterprise. The Missionary Album carried a list of 645 missionaries in active service, 29 per cent of whom were alumnae of the Training School. To get a true picture of that percentage, one has but to compare enrolment of the three seminaries with that of the Training School for that year, which was probably typical of the trend through the years, 2567 against 204. In other words, the School enrolled only 7 per cent of the total number of students in the four schools. To have trained 29 per cent of the active missionaries, therefore, was no mean accomplishment.

Imagine That!

One day during this period the principal went into the office and found a very puzzled student on duty at the desk. She had just received a call from some unknown lady who wanted to know if the School required the students to go out on the campus to pray! The unknown lady must have guessed that the student was dumbfounded at her question, so she hastened to explain that she had just driven by and had seen a student kneeling as if in prayer on the campus. The woman continued, "I thought it was sweet to see the girl praying, but I just wanted to know whether the School required it!"

The office girl told her that she didn't know what the girl was doing out on the front campus, but whatever it was, the School did not require it!

Later the mystery was solved when someone thought of Johnni Johnson, whose hobby was photography. She had been on the campus that morning and had taken several shots from a kneeling position! That unknown lady, however, probably still thinks there is something queer about that School!

A New Good Will Center

The Good Will Center Committee, with Mrs. E. M. Nuckols as chairman, had been carefully studying the underprivileged sections of Louisville for several years. In March, 1950, at the annual meeting of the Board of Trustees the committee recommended the purchase of property in the western part of the city. The century-old, well-preserved house was repaired and made ready for the opening in the fall. Miss Edith Vaughn, of Virginia, was secured as director. After two years she yielded to the pull of foreign missions and was appointed to direct a good will center in Brazil.

Miss Virginia Burke, of Georgia, succeeded Miss Vaughn as director of the Center. Talented in the field of art, she also teaches a popular course in arts and crafts at the School. The Good Will Center has had remarkable growth under her direction.

Organ Installed

At the homecoming in 1941 the Alumnae Association voted to install an organ in the chapel and made the initial contribution at that time. The fund grew slowly but steadily through the years. In 1948 the Executive Committee of the Association was authorized to proceed with definite plans for the purchase and installation.

In conference with Mr. Donald Winters and Mr. Kenneth Pool of the Seminary School of Music a contact was made with an unusual builder of organs, Mr. Walter Holtkamp, of Cleveland, Ohio. His method of installation, a return to the early European plan, solved the problem of space. Following many conferences the contract was given to Mr. Holtkamp in January, 1950.

In June, 1951, the organ was installed. Miss Claudia Edwards, music teacher at the School at that time, said, "For $9,580 one seldom, if ever, hears so much organ with such satisfying tone."

A New President for a New Era

After thirty years with the Training School Miss Littlejohn retired in 1951. Her work with the School had begun in 1921 when the student body had outgrown former provisions for teaching and guidance in field work. It had been a significant milestone in the progress of the School when the decision was made to secure a director for the Practical Missions Department. No work is more important in a professional school for leadership training, both secular and religious, than the program of supervised field work.

Realizing her need of more training in this field, the new director began spending her vacations in study in universities where there was opportunity for observing all types of settlement work, Hull House in Chicago, Henry Street Settlement in New York, and many smaller church settlements and Christian centers in Boston, New York, and Chicago.

Although Providence intervened within a few years and the direction of her service was changed, this special preparation could still be used in the total program of the School.

During thirty years of the School's forty-four she had been connected with it, including two years of rewarding service with Mrs. McLure, two years as acting principal following Mrs. McLure's retirement, five years of happy association with Mrs. Janie Cree Bose, and finally, principal and president from 1930 to 1951.

The Board of Trustees, sensing the direction that the School should take in the future, elected Miss Emily K. Landsdell, of Georgia, as the fourth head of the institution. She had many qualifications that fitted her admirably for this strategic position. She belonged to a family of religious and educational leaders. Her father, a graduate of the Seminary, had been connected with educational institutions through most of his life. Her mother, as a student wife, had attended Seminary classes before there was a school for women. In fact, she was one of those pioneer women who were admitted officially in 1903 to Seminary classes and allowed to take the examinations along with the men. She had been the first woman to take the examination in comparative religions and missions. Dr. Carver announced to the class that she had made the highest grade.

Miss Lansdell's educational preparation included a B.A. degree from Coker College, an M.A. degree in English from Duke University, and an M.A. in Oriental languages from Yale University. Prior to her appointment by the Foreign Mission Board she had studied part of a year in the Training School, then had gone to the University of California and Yale University for specific preparation for work in China. With splendid preparation in the best American universities and experience in teaching in Georgia high schools and Campbell College in North Carolina, Miss Lansdell was appointed to the University of Shanghai, where she taught for three years before conditions forced her to return to this country.

It would seem that this young woman, with her excellent preparation for missionary service and her actual participation in it, her personal dedication to missions and her progressive ideas as to the preparation needed, had "come to the kingdom for such a time as this."

At the opening of the session in Spetember, 1951, Miss Lansdell's inauguration was a happy event for the School. Mrs. George R. Martin, president of Woman's Missionary Union and chairman of the Board of Trustees, presided. Dr. W. O. Carver, the chief counselor and friend of the School from its earliest days, was there to lead in prayer. Dr. G. S. Dobbins, acting president of the Seminary, and Dr. Duke K. McCall, president-elect of the Seminary, brought greetings from the Southern Baptist Seminary. Miss Claudia Edwards spoke for the faculty and Miss Mary Pat Kent for the student body.

Dr. M. Theron Rankin, executive secretary of the Foreign Mission Board, introduced Miss Lansdell. He had known her as a student, as a teacher, as an appointee, and, finally, as a missionary.

In her excellent address Miss Lansdell justified the faith that had brought her to the School for a new era of service. She revealed a sympathetic understanding of the School's history and its contribution in many areas of denominational work. At the same time, she made a clear evaluation of the trend for the future. Keen observers realized with a thrill that under her leadership the School was now facing a new venture in its effort to fulfil its original missionary purpose. That purpose, envisioned in 1900 by Dr. Simmons, could now be worked out with intelligence and understanding as the School entered upon a new half century of adventure in missionary training.

A favorite hymn at the School in the early years was "God Is Working His Purpose Out." Those responsible for the School have not always clearly sensed the direction that it should take when a choice must be made, but they have been confident always that God is working his purpose out in and through this institution that has had so many evidences of divine guidance and blessing.

7

Unfinished Business

Our knowledge is a torch of smoky pine
That lights the pathway but one step ahead
Across a void of mystery and dread.
Bid, then, the tender light of faith to shine
By which alone the mortal heart is led
Unto the thinking of the thought divine.
                    GEORGE SANTAYANA [1]

THE FIRST PROBLEM to which Miss Lansdell and her faculty
gave serious attention was the direction that the School should
take in the immediate future. This was no new problem. For
at least two years it had been discussed many times by the
Training School faculty. It had been considered in a joint
meeting of the Training School faculty and the heads of departments at the Seminary. It had been brought to the attention of the Board of Trustees of the School in February, 1951.
From that day forward both the faculty and the Board were
compelled to give this matter their major consideration.

The Purpose Redefined

Such a problem arose because of the desire and need on the
part of the Seminary to develop its department of religious
education into a school for the training of both men and
women for the educational field. Due to the growth of the
denomination and the consequent development of the program
for the local church, there was the demand for educational
directors. In order to meet professional standards, the de-

partment must be developed into a school with an adequate curriculum.

This situation posed a problem for both schools, for they had worked together in fine co-operation to prepare women for church work on the local level, particularly in those periods when there were few opportunities for direct mission work open to women. Dr. Weatherspoon expressed the concern of the Seminary in his Founders' Day address in October, 1956:

> This Seminary held back for years and years. It determined that there must be no competition between the Training School and the seminary. But the day came when both the seminary and the Training School realized that the seminary must have for both men and women a school of religious education. The day came, therefore, through the inevitable pressure of denominational growth and the expansion of functions, when the question arose concerning the future of the Training School.[2]

The Training School administration was likewise deeply concerned over this unforeseen development. As the problem was studied, three solutions appeared to be possible. First of all, the School could be merged with the Seminary and become the school of religious education. As this possibility was considered, it did not seem to offer the best solution. Would Woman's Missionary Union be justified in going into the business of maintaining a school of religious education for one seminary? Would it be morally acceptable to divert the missionary investment of fifty years out of the channel of direct missions?

Another course was open. Woman's Missionary Union could consider its work completed in this area of training for missions, close the doors of the School, sell the property, and redirect the investment to mission causes that would be acceptable both legally and morally.

As the knotty problem was studied, a third way out suggested itself. After all, in the light of its original purpose, was

the work of the School completed? Again Dr. Weatherspoon
clarified the issue as he put into words the deep convictions
that had motivated the decisions about the future of the
School. In the address quoted above he said:

Then someone began to ask questions—questions about what the
function of the Training School was in the first place. It was to
supply something that wasn't being done, something that was necessary, something big enough to challenge the people of the south
to a new venture.

And in the light of that purpose people began to make answer
as they surveyed our whole Christian education program as a Convention. . . . somebody called attention to the fact that we are in
a new day of missionary advance. . . . today we have more than
a thousand home missionaries. And the Foreign Board is thinking
in terms of an early 1,750 and then as many as 2,000. That is to say,
the missionary work of the Southern Baptist Convention is on the
march.

Into new fields, with new functions, with a new vision of the demands upon the men and women who go.[3]

And so by 1952 conclusions had been reached by both the
Seminary and the Training School. The Seminary announced
that the School of Religious Education would be opened in the
fall of 1953, pending final approval of the plan by the Seminary
Board of Trustees.

Recognizing the fact that the School's purpose and function
had been undergoing changes and adjustments all through
the years in the light of world needs and opportunities, the
administration of the Training School accepted this challenge
to its resourcefulness. Its work in the beginning had been pioneer work in the field of missionary training. Why not pioneer
again in a field not yet entered by the denomination. The way
could again be opened by women.

Two areas were still untouched by any Southern Baptist
school or seminary—advanced and specialized training for the
foreign missionary and a social work program for training for

173

home missions with special emphasis on city missions, good will centers, children's homes, and homes for the aged.

A New Direction

All through the fall and winter of her first year Miss Lansdell and her faculty studied these undeveloped areas of missionary preparation and visualized a school of missions and Christian social work. The seminaries were giving basic courses in missions, but after all, these schools were designed to train men for a pastoral ministry, and that in itself is a large order in the light of the needs of the modern church.

When the Board of Trustees met in Louisville in February, 1952, Miss Lansdell brought the faculty findings to this group for consideration. On this matter, and on every proposed development until his death, Dr. Carver's guidance was also sought. The Board carefully weighed the implications of such a step and came to the conclusion that the time was ripe for the establishing of a school of missions and Christian social work.

In the light of the great missionary advance, the need was apparent. If the women of fifty years ago, with their limited resources, could venture on faith to initiate a school of missions, surely the women of today with their rich resources could take their venture of faith and build on the priceless heritage something worthy of today's opportunities.

Accordingly, the Board of Trustees formulated recommendations which were presented to Woman's Missionary Union at the annual meeting in Miami in May, 1952. These recommendations, adopted by the body, turned the School definitely in a new direction, in which the major emphasis would be on missions and church social work. To bolster this pioneer program, a larger appropriation would be needed from the Cooperative Program, which in turn would provide for additions to the faculty and other needed developments in the program of advance.

A New Name

One of the intriguing plans in the historic 1952 meeting of the Board of Trustees committed the body to change the name of the School. This was not a new idea. It had been suggested as early as 1924. From time to time it had been discussed in the years that followed.

It had been evident for a long time that the title "Training School" was outmoded for a school of this type. It had come into use in the field of social work as a name for the old style reformatory. It had also been adopted by the local church as a designation for the church-wide program for training teachers. A new name was long overdue, but time and again in the recurring discussion no suggestion had ever caught the imagination of the group. This time it was different. There was nothing vacillating in the decision of the Board in 1952. The name was to be changed. Everybody would be given a chance to make suggestions. The choice of a new name would be made in 1953.

Mrs. Martin, in her role as chairman of the Board of Trustees, knew that this would be an epoch-making meeting. Guidance and inspiration must be sought for the far-reaching steps to be taken in a new direction. The needed help was close at hand in the person of Dr. W. O. Carver, the great missionary statesman and the School's most valuable friend. To sound the keynote of this meeting, therefore, Dr. Carver was asked to speak at a convocation of the trustees, faculty, and student body. In reporting this address, Miss Mary J. Augenstein said, "With vigor, enthusiasm and the scholarly perception that has characterized his life and work, he envisioned a program of preparation that would be needed for the world mission task fifty years hence. He suggested as a name for the institution providing such training, 'The School of World Christianity.'" [4]

The keynote had been sounded. World missions—a world outlook—world Christianity—preparation of missionaries commensurate with the tremendous undertaking—the original purpose had been clarified, magnified, and glorified!

Inspired, humbled, and stimulated, the Board went into two days of strenuous conference. The last session came, with the decision as to the name still to be made. The chairman called for suggestions. There must have been a moment of silence, then someone (the records do not name the person) suggested "Carver School of Missions and Social Work." That idea kindled the imagination as nothing else had! In the sequence of events God's time was now ripe for a new emphasis on an old purpose, and a new name, this name, would leave no doubt as to the direction in which the School was going.

When Mrs. Carver learned that the Alumni Association planned to present a portrait of Dr. Carver to the School, she did a most generous thing in offering to give the portrait painted in 1938. At the opening convocation in September, 1953, the portrait was presented, with the two sons living in Louisville, Professor George Carver and W. O. Carver, Jr., participating, and Mrs. Carver making the presentation speech. Her delightful brand of humor sparkled through the speech. At the same time, her mastery of pathos, so sincere and unstudied, brought a quick tear and a catch in the throat.

Today as the visitor enters the lobby of the building he sees on the right wall facing the door the portrait of Mrs. McLure and on the left that of Dr. Carver, the two personalities who have without question made the most lasting contributions to the School.

Faith's Blueprint

When Dr. Carver delivered his challenging address in February, 1953, at the special convocation called by Mrs. Martin in connection with the meeting of the Board of Trustees, he outlined a curriculum for his idea of a school of world Christianity that could serve as a pattern for years to come.

After Woman's Missionary Union approved the program of

advance outlined by the Board of Trustees, Miss Lansdell and the Executive Committee of the Board promptly began to work out the details. In line with Dr. Carver's forward-looking suggestions, expanding the curriculum by enlarging the faculty was the first step on their schedule. Within the year Dr. Hugh A. Brimm was named professor of sociology and human relations and Mr. George A. Carver, professor of missions.

The policy of securing a missionary every year as a visiting professor in the Department of Missions was adopted. The following men have served on the faculty under this policy: Dr. Maxfield Garrott, of Japan, in 1952–1953; Dr. Lavell Seats, of Nigeria, in 1953–1954; Dr. John Allen Moore, of Yugoslavia, in 1954–1955; Dr. A. R. Crabtree, of Brazil, in 1955–1956; and Dr. J. Glenn Morris, of Thailand, in 1956–1957.

In the field of social work similar developments have been taking place. Several part-time teachers, whose courses have greatly enriched the curriculum, have been added to the faculty.

In addition to the expanding curriculum in Carver School, students still have access to any classes in the Seminary schools of theology, music, and religious education.

As the faculty has grown in these new directions, there have been the inevitable losses that come to any institution as workers feel led to go into other fields of service. Such a loss came in the resignation of Miss Claudia Edwards in 1954 to give her full time to her major interest, teaching public school music.

Miss Edwards has many interests, and she has had the opportunity to explore them all during the twenty-seven years she was on the faculty of the School. In a small school it is difficult for a staff or faculty member to confine himself to one job. There is usually a combination of two related or even two totally different avenues of service. For some this is interesting, for others very difficult. Whether easy or difficult for her, Miss Edwards has had many combinations, but music was always one of them. At different periods during her years at the School

177

she combined with music work at the Good Will Center, supervision of field work, and finally, the office of alumnae secretary.

Miss Miriam Robinson said of Miss Edwards:

Perhaps her greatest contribution to the School was her consistent friendliness to faculty, students, and servants equally . . . Her love for people and keen insight into their needs were quickly translated into very practical action. . . . She always had time for people: to run an errand for the dietitian, to listen to the little daughter of a Seminary student play her first piano piece, to teach music to a little Chinese girl in the city, to talk to students in the hall, to show visitors over the building, . . . to help students with a special program.[5]

In 1955 Miss Robinson resigned to go back into Woman's Missionary Union work as executive secretary in North Carolina. Her major work in the School since 1944 had been teaching speech and dramatics. She combined with that work assistance in supervising field work and during her last year, some teaching in missionary education. Her charm as a person, her ability as a teacher, and her example as a radiant Christian made her a favorite among her students.

An enlarged faculty called for more classroom and office space and a larger library. After studying the School's capital needs, the Southern Baptist Convention voted to give $320,000 for an addition to the present building to house the library and the needed classrooms and offices. Further expansion was made possible by the purchase of the fourteen-room colonial residence next door to the campus.

In 1952 the trustees voted to admit students without regard to race or nationality. The first Nigerian student, Mrs. Adeola Adegbite, enrolled for the 1952–1953 session while her husband was studying at the Seminary.

In 1952 the Board also voted to admit men to the classes, though the School was not prepared to house them. This situation, coupled with the aversion of the average man to enrolling in an institution managed by women, has deterred men from taking advantage of the opportunities offered at Carver. A few have enrolled, however, and two have been graduated by the School. Louis Stone, of Oklahoma, received the M.R.E. degree in 1955, and Rufus H. Fisher, of South Carolina, the same degree in 1956. Both men were interested in children's homes. Mr. Stone is on the staff of the Missouri Baptist Children's Home and Mr. Fisher of Connie Maxwell Children's Home in South Carolina.

No point in the program of advance projected in 1952 has been neglected. The faculty and the Board of Trustees have been working on the plan, step by step, and they have reason to be gratified because of the progress made.

The Death of Dr. Carver

With the death of Dr. Carver on May 24, 1954, the last link with the early days of the School was broken. He had been a student in the Seminary in 1891–1893 and again in 1895–1896. He had made a brilliant record, earning the Th.M. and Th.D. degrees in three and a half years. Recognizing his promise as a teacher, the faculty asked him to stay on at the Seminary as instructor in New Testament and homiletics. In 1898 he was elected by the Board of Trustees as assistant professor.

With his keen mind and devoted missionary spirit, he was always thinking ahead of his contemporaries. In a rearrangement of courses at the Seminary in 1899 he pioneered in the field of theological education by introducing a course in comparative religion and missions. At that time there was only one other school, the University of Halle in Germany, which had such a course.

As a student in the Seminary he observed the women who came to classes with their husbands. As a teacher he gave them sympathetic attention and encouraged them to feel that they were welcome. As the occasional unmarried woman shyly drifted into the classes, he was even more concerned about her. Some of them had written to him for advice about coming to the Seminary, sensing somehow before they knew him that he would have a personal interest in them and their desire for training.

He was there at the turn of the century when Dr. Simmons went to Louisville to discuss with the faculty the idea of starting a training school for women. That idea found a ready response in Dr. Carver's heart.

When the faculty planned the special course in practical missions for women students, it was natural that they should turn to Dr. Carver to teach it. They knew his interest in missions and had observed that he was never too busy to give his attention to these struggling young women. Occasionally when they ran into financial difficulties, he made it possible for them to continue their studies.

In the providence of God, it was he who noticed the four, known as the "Big Four," in 1904. Concerned about their living arrangements, he conferred with Miss Broadus, who set in motion the movement that provided a home for them.

In 1907 when the little school was adopted by Woman's Missionary Union, he was asked to be a member of the Advisory Committee, and through the years until his death he continued to serve the School in that official capacity. Through the difficult early years, through changes of administration, through reverses and advance, he was always there, the School's best friend and most trusted counselor.

With humility and gratitude, faculty, students, and friends who had gathered in Heck Memorial Chapel on Founders' Day in 1948 heard him conclude his great address with these words: "May I be excused for saying in a final word that I account the privilege of having been associated in some measure with the beginnings and the continuance of this School through nearly half a century one of the highest honors God has given me in his great grace."

The Death of Miss Mallory

Another beloved friend of the School, Miss Kathleen Mallory, passed from the earthly stage of action shortly after Dr. Carver's death. Following an illness of several months, she died June 17, 1954, in Selma, Alabama, the city that she called home. She loved Woman's Missionary Union because it was a channel for service to world missions, beginning with her own personal witnessing and extending to the ends of the earth. She loved Carver School of Missions because it was a channel for missions through which she and every member of the Union could reach every area of missionary need. For thirty-six years she had been a member of the Board of Trustees, and no member ever served it more lovingly and loyally. Her annual visits to the School were stimulating experiences for faculty and students alike. Her attractive personality, her charm as a conversationalist, her devotion to missions, and her singleness of purpose as a Christian left an indelible impression on everyone who was privileged to touch her life.

Major Changes in 1956

Mrs. George R. Martin chose to retire as the president of Woman's Missionary Union in this momentous year. For eleven years in utter forgetfulness of personal interests she had "poured out the resources and vitality of body, mind, and heart" in the interest of the worldwide work of the Union. One of these interests had been Carver School of Missions and Social Work. As chairman of its Board of Trustees she was called on to guide the Board through the School's major transition period.

Through these difficult years she endeared herself to the Board and faculty alike through her fair and considerate approach to every question. The meeting of the Executive Committee of the Board of Trustees in early May of the last year of her administration gave Louisville friends an opportunity to honor Mrs. Martin at a dinner in the School dining room. During the dinner hour a group of students under the direction of Miss Elaine Neeley presented a program depicting significant events in Mrs. Martin's life.

Mrs. R. L. Mathis, of Texas, succeeded Mrs. Martin as president of Woman's Missionary Union. Coming into her office as ex officio chairman of the Board of Trustees at this time of transition in the School's life, it was fortunate that she was thoroughly conversant with recent developments and was concerned with helping guide the School into its new role as a distinctive graduate school in missions and social work.

In line with the new program of advance, the first summer session of the School was launched in 1956. An interesting course of study was planned for missionaries under appointment, those on furlough, church social workers, WMU leaders, and other denominational workers. Some outstanding visiting teachers joined the regular members of the Carver School faculty to make this first summer session a notable one. Mr. Richard Cortright, of World Literacy, Inc., of New York, and Mr. Robert Laubach, of the University of Syracuse, taught classes in literacy techniques, phonetics, and the teaching of English as a foreign language.

Golden Anniversary Year

The 1956–1957 session brought Carver School of Missions to its half-century milestone. Well in advance of this history-making year, plans were set in motion by Woman's Missionary Union to celebrate this fiftieth anniversary in a worthy way. Mrs. Martin appointed a large anniversary committee, made up of state WMU presidents, executive secretaries and youth secretaries, with Mrs. R. L. Mathis as chairman, to outline and project the program.

A number of special programs were featured at the School during the year so that the students might share in the inspiration of the anniversary. The first of these programs was

Founders' Day, observed on Monday, October 1, 1956, with Dr. J. B. Weatherspoon, professor of homiletics at the Seminary, as the speaker. He made a unique address on the subject, "The Adventures of a Purpose."

Monday, October 29, was dedicated to "Southern Baptists and World Missions." The panel of speakers included Dr. Baker J. Cauthen, Dr. George W. Sadler, Dr. James W. Crawley, Mr. Elmer S. West, Jr., and Miss Edna Frances Dawkins, all from the Foreign Mission Board.

Other special programs included "Training for World Christian Service" on February 11, "Opportunities and Training for Church Social Work" on March 18, and a Young Woman's Auxiliary houseparty on April 19–21.

An event of special interest to former students was homecoming, held in connection with the anniversary commencement, May 22–24, 1957. Louise Smith Boyd (Mrs. D. F.), alumni president, and her committee had prepared a schedule that kept even the most youthful going breathlessly from early morning until late at night. The program was well balanced between inspiration and fun, history and tradition, activity and reminiscence.

The fiftieth anniversary service on Wednesday evening was the first and the most inspiring of the series of services. Mr. Gordon Flesher at the organ and the Carver choir, under the direction of Ruth Garcia McElrath (Mrs. H. T.), maintained the mood of worship throughout the service. The pageant, directed by Norma Jean Baker, reviewed the blessings of the past and called to a new dedication for the future. In the pageant the founders were vividly portrayed by Mrs. George R. Ferguson as Miss Eliza Broadus; Mrs. Heber Peacock as Mrs. S. E. Woody; Miss Rose Marlowe as Mrs. George B. Eager; Miss Mary Julia Augenstein as Miss Heck; and Miss Hannah Reynolds as Mrs. McLure.

The "Fiftieth Anniversary Hymn" served as the introduction to the pageant. Mrs. W. O. Carver wrote the words for this hymn especially for this occasion. The music was composed by Dr. Donald Packard, formerly on the faculty of the Seminary School of Church Music.

The anniversary commencement on Thursday morning was a time of inspiration for the 1957 graduates, as Mrs. R. L. Mathis pointed out the major choices that they must make. It was a time of remembering for many former graduates and a time of gratitude for the unmeasured blessings that had come to them through the ministry of their Alma Mater.

Following the commencement service former students and friends went to the Seelbach Hotel for a luncheon program and business meeting. Under the theme, "Through Golden Doors," the speakers pointed to the golden yesterday as but an introduction to the beckoning future. Fun, good food, and fellowship were interspersed with the more serious moments of the occasion.

On Thursday evening following a worship service led by Miss Miriam Robinson, a portrait of Miss Carrie U. Littlejohn was presented to the School by Miss Mary Northington on behalf of the Alumni Association.

From the chapel the group went to the recreation room for a fun session led by Miss Georgie Fancher, Miss Dorothy Pryor, and Mrs. David F. Boyd. The closing event was a fun-filled breakfast hour in the dining room on Friday morning directed by Mrs. Agnes Durant Pylant.

The climax of the anniversary year was the observance of the Semicentennial of Carver School at a luncheon in Medinah Temple in Chicago on May 28 during the 1957 annual meeting of Woman's Missionary Union. Several hundred guests, including former students, denominational leaders, and friends of the School, gathered around the beautifully decorated tables to enjoy this memorable occasion. Mrs. George R. Martin, presiding at the luncheon program, presented Miss Littlejohn and Miss Lansdell, who spoke briefly, and Mrs. H. T. McElrath, who led the ensemble of the Carver School choir in the special music. The main address was delivered by Dr. Paul Geren, executive vice-president of Baylor University, who formerly served with the State Department in the Middle East.

A New Venture of Faith

The new direction that was marked out for the School in 1952 by the Board of Trustees called for major changes. It is possible that this group of women did not fully comprehend at that time how far-reaching these changes would be. They only knew that they were acting in accordance with what they believed to be God's leading. In taking one step they found light for the next one.

In January, 1952, President Emily Lansdell said in her report to the Executive Board of Woman's Missionary Union that it was her conviction that the proposed venture at the School would need the backing of the entire Southern Baptist Convention.

In February, 1953, Dr. Carver said in his historic address at a special convocation at the School:

The Woman's Missionary Union Training School . . . can serve as the initiating and organizing center for a new venture in this field of higher education for leadership in the new demands of a new age.

. . . Such a school cannot meet the need as a school for women alone, or even primarily. The entire Convention, in all its agencies, needs such a school. Men and women leaders are already needed and will be needed in increasing numbers. Meeting such a need will require the sympathy, the thought, the direction, and the support of the entire constituency of the Southern Baptist Convention.[6]

In line with the program of advance planned by the Board of Trustees in February, 1952, the request was presented to the Finance Committee of the Executive Committee of the Southern Baptist Convention in December of that year for 1½ per cent of the distributable funds in the Cooperative Program for the operating budget of Carver School. The request

185

was denied because the School was not an agency of the Convention. Since it was evident by this time that the whole situation needed clarification, a committee was appointed by the Executive Committee of the Convention to study the relationship of the School to the Southern Baptist Convention.

This committee, of which Dr. W. Douglas Hudgins was chairman, met in Louisville early in 1953 to begin its study. The following May the Southern Baptist Convention appointed a committee to study the total program of theological, religious, and missionary education of the denomination. In its study this committee gave much attention to Carver School and its relationship to the Convention. The committee met again and again and conferred often with WMU leaders and Miss Lansdell.

In 1955 the Convention instructed this committee to study in particular the financial relationship of Carver School to the Convention and make recommendations concerning future relationships. A subcommittee, with Dr. Herschel Hobbs as chairman, was appointed to make this study. As the committee continued its work, they requested that representatives from Woman's Missionary Union join them in formulating the recommendations to be presented to the Convention in 1956. Mrs. George R. Martin appointed Miss Alma Hunt, executive secretary of the Union, Mrs. Horace Hammett from the Carver Board of Trustees, Dr. Olin Binkley from the Carver Advisory Committee, and President Emily Lansdell to serve with her on this joint committee.

From this committee the recommendation concerning Carver School went to the larger committee on theological education, which in turn presented it to the Convention at the annual meeting in 1956. This recommendation as adopted by the Convention provided that Carver School of Missions would be accepted as an institution of the Southern Baptist Convention, operating within the business and financial plan of the Convention, as soon as Woman's Missionary Union changed its by-laws so that the Carver School trustees could be elected by the Convention.

The WMU Executive Board and the Carver School Board of Trustees explored from every angle the implications of this recommendation. Since 1952 each step in the new direction had been taken in prayer and faith. Now this major change appeared as the next step in faith's blueprint. In confidence, therefore, the WMU Executive Board recommended to Woman's Missionary Union that the support and control of Carver School of Missions and Social Work be transferred to the Southern Baptist Convention. The recommendation was adopted without discussion.

The year that followed was a busy one for the Woman's Missionary Union committee as they worked with the Convention committee in planning the transfer so as to safeguard the investments and trust funds of Carver School. In this complicated business they had the best legal guidance. In accepting Mrs. Martin's report on Monday, May 27, 1957, Woman's Missionary Union gave its full approval to the transfer of the School.

On Wednesday, May 29, the Committee on Theological Education made its report to the Southern Baptist Convention. The major recommendation in that report was that the control, ownership, and maintenance of Carver School be transferred from Woman's Missionary Union to the Southern Baptist Convention. When the Convention adopted the recommendation, a new era began for this beloved institution.

A Birmingham newspaper on August 14, 1956, featured the picture of the remains of a burned old mansion with nothing left except the stately columns and the substantial chimneys clearly silhouetted against the Alabama sky. Underneath the picture was the caption, "The end of a symbol." The day before, lightning had struck "Mount Ida," and the beautiful old home, featured in many magazines as one of the show places of the South, had burned to the ground—"Mount Ida," the birthplace of Maud Reynolds McLure, a symbol of the life and work of other days, and now "the end of a symbol." But there is something left, something that speaks of beauty, warmth, stability, and permanence.

As Carver School of Missions and Social Work passed from the fostering care of Woman's Missionary Union to become one of the schools of higher learning supported by the Southern Baptist Convention, one could have been tempted to think, "This, too, is the end of a symbol." On second thought, however, there was the realization that as the beloved School goes under new sponsorship, it takes with it some things that cannot be destroyed: the beautiful memory of investments of personality, priceless in its contribution, and of gifts, often sacrificial, that have built and maintained the School for half a century; the warmth of a blessed fellowship among its former students in service around the world; the stability of the continued love and concern of the women who are, after all, a part of the Convention; and the permanence of its abiding missionary purpose.

Notes

Chapter 1

1. Kenneth Scott Latourette, *Missions Tomorrow* (New York: Harper & Brothers, 1936), p. 5.
2. *Baptist Argus* (Louisville), January 3, 1907, p. 4.
3. Kenneth Scott Latourette, *The Emergence of a World Christian Community* (New Haven: Yale University Press, 1949), p. 11.
4. Arthur Judson Brown, *The Why and How of Foreign Missions* (New York: Young People's Missionary Movement of the United States and Canada, 1908), pp. 256–7.
5. Vera Brittain, *Lady into Woman* (New York: Macmillan Co., 1953), p. 8.
6. William Owen Carver, "Christ's Gift to Women," *Review and Expositor*, XXXVIII (July, 1941), 259.
7. *Ibid.*, p. 254.
8. *Christian Index* (Atlanta), March 29, 1906, p. 1.
9. Mimeographed copy of "Statement." Historical Scrapbook, Carver School.
10. Minutes of the Woman's Missionary Union Executive Committee, November 12, 1895.
11. Letter to Miss Armstrong. Historical Scrapbook.
12. Minutes of the Woman's Missionary Union Executive Committee, April 10, 1900.
13. *Christian Index* (Atlanta), February 22, 1906, p. 6.
14. Mimeographed copy of "Statement."
15. *Report of the Fifteenth Annual Meeting of the Woman's Missionary Union*, 1903, p. 21.
16. *Baptist Argus* (Louisville), April 7, 1904, p. 1.
17. *Ibid.*, May 5, 1904, p. 9.
18. *Ibid.*, May 19, 1904, p. 8.
19. *Report of the Sixteenth Annual Meeting of the Woman's Missionary Union*, 1904, p. 44.

20. *Christian Index* (Atlanta), May 19, 1904, p. 4.
21. *Annual of the Southern Baptist Convention*, 1904, p. 5.
22. *Christian Index* (Atlanta), May 19, 1904, p. 4.
23. *Baptist Argus* (Louisville), April 21, 1904, p. 5.
24. *Baptist and Reflector* (Nashville), August 4, 1904, p. 3.
25. *Baptist Argus* (Louisville), September 22, 1904, p. 6.
26. *Ibid.*, August 24, 1905, p. 6.
27. *Ibid.*, May 11, 1905, p. 4.
28. Letter to the "Investigation Committee of Virginia," February 29, 1906. Historical Scrapbook.
29. *Report of the Seventeenth Annual Meeting of the Woman's Missionary Union*, 1905, p. 28.
30. *Christian Index* (Atlanta), May 25, 1905, p. 2.
31. *Ibid.*, May 25, 1905, p. 2.
32. *Baptist Argus* (Louisville), May 25, 1905, p. 6
33. *Report of the Seventeenth Annual Meeting of the Woman's Missionary Union*, 1905, p. 40.
34. *Baptist Argus* (Louisville), May 25, 1905, p. 6.
35. *Annual of the Southern Baptist Convention*, 1905, p. 24.
36. Minutes of the Woman's Missionary Union Executive Committee, May 25, 1905.
37. Minutes of the Woman's Missionary Union Executive Committee, October 10, 1905.
38. Minutes of the Woman's Missionary Union Executive Committee, October 16, 1905.
39. Minutes of the Woman's Missionary Union Executive Committee, February 13, 1906.
40. Minutes of the Woman's Missionary Union Executive Committee, April 10, 1906
41. Minutes of the Woman's Missionary Union Executive Committee, April 10, 1906.
42. *Report of the Eighteenth Annual Meeting of the Woman's Missionary Union*, 1906, p. 49.
43. *Ibid.*
44. Minutes of the Woman's Missionary Union Executive Committee, March 4, 1907.

Chapter 2

1. Isla May Mullins, *House Beautiful* (Nashville: The Sunday School Board of the Southern Baptist Convention, 1934), p. 26.
2. *Baptist Argus* (Louisville), October 10, 1907, p. 1.

3. Historical Scrapbook.
4. Mullins, *op. cit.*, p. 32.
5. *Baptist Courier* (Greenville, South Carolina), May 25, 1916, p. 8.
6. *Baptist Advance* (Little Rock), June 8, 1916, p. 7.
7. *Baptist Standard* (Dallas), June 15, 1916, p. 10.

Chapter 3

1. *Report of the Thirty-seventh Annual Meeting of Woman's Missionary Union,* 1921, p. 91.
2. *Report of the Forty-first Annual Meeting of Woman's Missionary Union,* 1925, p. 93.
3. *Royal Service,* XIX (July, 1925), 30.

Chapter 4

1. *Religious Herald* (Richmond), June 19, 1930, p. 14.
2. *Royal Service,* XXV (November, 1931), 31.
3. *Royal Service,* XXV (December, 1931), 5.
4. *Royal Service,* XXVII (September, 1933), 18–19.
5. Ethel Winfield, "Training School Has First Founders' Day." Historical Scrapbook.
6. *Report of the Forty-ninth Annual Meeting of Woman's Missionary Union,* 1937, pp. 72–73.

Chapter 5

1. Minutes of the Board of Trustees of Woman's Missionary Union Training School, October 1–3, 1936.
2. *Western Recorder* (Louisville), June 24, 1937, p. 20.
3. *Report of the Fiftieth Annual Meeting of the Woman's Missionary Union,* 1938, pp. 107–111.
4. *Report of the Fifty-second Annual Meeting of Woman's Missionary Union,* 1940, p. 83.
5. *Report of the Fifty-first Annual Meeting of Woman's Missionary Union,* 1939, p. 80.
6. *Royal Service,* XXXIV (May, 1940), 11.
7. *Royal Service,* XXXV (July, 1941), 6.

Chapter 6

1. Mrs. F. W. Armstrong, "Lighted to Lighten," Historical Scrapbook.
2. *Ibid.*
3. *W.M.U. Training School Bulletin,* July, 1948, p. 7.

4. *Report of Meeting of Fifty-eighth Year of Woman's Missionary Union*, 1946, p. 3.
5. *Ibid.*, p. 3.
6. Minutes of the Woman's Missionary Union Executive Committee, April 11, 1945.
7. Minutes of the Woman's Missionary Union Executive Committee, April 11, 1945.

Chapter 7

1. From *Poems* (New York: Charles Scribner's Sons, 1923). Used by permission.
2. Jesse B. Weatherspoon, "Adventures of a Purpose," Historical Scrapbook.
3. *Ibid.*
4. *Alumni Bulletin*, July, 1953, p. 3.
5. *Alumni Bulletin*, December, 1954, p. 2.
6. William Owen Carver, "If I Were under Thirty." Historical Scrapbook.

Faculty and Staff 1907–1957

Mrs. Maud Reynolds McLurc	Principal	1907–23
Miss Emma Leachman	Applied Methods in City Missions	1907–21
Miss Julia McIver	Piano and Organ	1907–09
Miss Lois Downer	Elocution	1907–09
Miss Ellen Brown	Domestic Science	1907–09
Miss Evelyn Gardner	Piano and Organ	1909–12
Miss Hallie Mosby	Resident Nurse	1909–10
Mrs. B. H. DeMent	Mission Study	1910–12
Mrs. Effie N. Amerine	Housekeeper	1910–13
Dr. Julia Ingram	Principles of Medicine	1910–19
Mrs. George B. Eager	Mission Study	1912–22
	Financial Secretary	1919–22
	Financial Sec. & Treas.	1922–26
	WMU Course	1922–23
Miss Lucile Humphreys	Piano and Organ	1912–14
Miss Evie Wade	Physical Director	1912–13
Miss Nona Lee Dover	Elocution	1912–13
Miss Ada Coombs	Resident Nurse	1912–27
Mrs. Katherine W. Dobbs	Sight Singing	1913–14
Miss Anna Abbett	Office Secretary	1913–17
Mrs. W. H. Tharpe	Expression	1913–18
Mrs. Lila T. Inman	Housekeeper	1913–14
Miss Gertrude Tucker	Piano	1914–15
Miss Mary Mitchell	Housekeeper	1914–20
	House Director and Dietitian	1936–48
Mrs. Lillie L. Albany	Music	1917–20

Miss Lizzie Graham	Office Secretary	1917–18
Mrs. G. J. Sutterlin	Public Speaking	1918–42
Miss Pearl Conner	Office Secretary	1921–30
Miss Carrie U. Littlejohn	Director of Practical Missions	1921–31
	Acting Principal	1923–25
	Associate Principal	1925–31
	Principal and President	1931–51
Dr. Alice N. Pickett	Principles of Medicine	1921–22
Dr. Annie S. Veech	Principles of Medicine	1921–22
Miss Mary L. Warren	House Director and Dietitian	1921–36
Miss Ruby Quillin	Asst. Director Good Will Center	1923–24
Miss Alice Johnson	Asst. Director Good Will Center	1924–26
Miss Wilma Bucy	W. M. U. Course	1924–27
Mrs. Janie Cree Bose	Principal	1925–30
Mrs. E. A. McDowell, Jr.	Music	1925–29
Miss Helen Gibson	Asst. House Director	1925–26
Dr. C. L. McGinty	Bible	1925–36
Miss Latta Greer	Treasurer	1926–36
Miss Claudia Edwards	Music and Good Will Center	
	Music and Director of Field Work	
	Music and Alumnae Sec'y	1926–54
Miss Hannah Reynolds	WMU Course	1927–28
Miss Eva Sanders	Physical Education	
	Asst. Director Good Will Center	1927–28
Miss Velma Dillman	Resident Nurse	1927–29
Miss Elsie Ragsdale	Missionary Education	1928–38
Miss Eva Brewer	Resident Nurse	1929–41
Miss Ruth Maness	Office Sec'y; Registrar	1930–38
Miss Elizabeth Hale	Asst. at Good Will Center	1930–32
Miss Frances Curb	Asst. at Good Will Center	1935–38

Miss Anna Murchison	Office Sec'y; Registrar	1938–42
Miss Wanda Lynch	Director of Good Will Center	1938–41
Miss Georgie Fancher	Librarian	1938–
Miss Mary Christian	Missionary Education	1939–41
Miss Mary Nelle Lyne	Missionary Education	1941–46
Mrs. J. F. Smith	Resident Nurse	1941–44
Miss Anne Tennant	Speech Physical Education	1942–44
Miss Virginia Bean	Office Secretary Registrar Office Practice	1942–46
Miss Ruth Boone	Journalism	1942–44
Miss Mary Ellen Wooten	Supervisor of Field Work	1944–46
Mrs. O. L. Judy	Asst. House Director	1944–46
Miss Miriam Robinson	Speech and Dramatics	1944–55
Miss Virginia Wingo	Missionary Education	1946–49
Miss Eva Dawson	House Director Dietitian	1946–50 1950–
Miss Josephine Huddleston	Social Work	1947–48
Miss Elaine Neeley	Office Secretary Missionary Education Financial Secretary	1947–57
Miss Bertha Sexton	Dietitian	1948–50
Miss Velma Darbo	Registrar Secretary to President	1948–50
Miss Martha Hairston	Director of Field Work Social Work	1949–51
Mrs. Peter Kittles	House Director	1950–51
Miss Florence Ritter	Office Secretary	1950–53
Miss Martha Richardson	Registrar Secretary to President	1950–53
Miss Mary J. Augenstein	Field Representative Alumnae Secretary	1950–56
Miss Edith Vaughn	Director of Good Will Center	1950–53
Miss Kathryn Bigham	Director of Field Work Social Work	1951–

Miss Emily K. Lansdell	President	1951–58
Dr. Maxfield Garrott	Missions	1952–53
Mrs. Mary Crouch	House Director	1952–
Dr. Samuel J. Anderson	Medical Information	1953–57
Dr. Hugh Brimm	Sociology and Human Relations	1953–
Mr. George A. Carver	Missions	1953–
Miss Virginia Burke	Director of Good Will Center	
	Arts and Crafts	1953–
Dr. Grace Chen	Phonetics and Linguistics	1953–55
Dr. Lavell Seats	Missions	1953–54
Mr. Donald C. Harvey	Social Group Work	1953–55
Miss Esther Dixon	Secretary to President	1953–56
Dr. Robert J. Lehman	Psychiatric Information	
	Development of Personality	1954–
Dr. John Allen Moore	Missions	1954–55
Dr. Frank Vicroy	Community Organization	1954–
Miss Mary Lee Rankin	Advisor to Students	1954–55
Mrs. Marshall Flournoy	Secretary to Faculty	1954–55
Mrs. Hugh McElrath	Music	1954–
Dr. A. R. Crabtree	Missions	1955–56
Mrs. David Stull	Speech and Dramatics	1955–
Mrs. Dan Stringer	Secretary to Faculty	1955–
Mrs. Roger Benton	Asst. Director Good Will Center	1955–56
Mr. Buford E. Farris, Jr.	Social Group Work	1956–
Miss Elizabeth Gross	Social Group Work	1956–
Dr. J. Glenn Morris	Missions	1956–57
Mr. A. L. Taylor	Law and Social Work	1956–
Mr. Roger Benton	Asst. Director Good Will Center	1956–
Miss Norma Jean Baker	Asst. in Public Relations	1956–
Mrs. B. F. Loyd	Secretary to President	1956–

196

Hymns

See thy children rise with blessing;
  Far and near their voices raising;
Clasping hands across the waters;
  Pledged to serve through endless days.
To the Lord thy sons and daughters
  Give the glory and the praise.

To thy door God's mercy led us;
  Truth and wisdom thou hast fed us;
Op'ed our eyes to see the glory
  And the wonder of His face;
Loosed our tongues to tell His story;
  Tuned our hearts to sing His grace.

Gentle spirit, born of Heaven,
  Guiding light, divinely given,
Kindle fresh thy life within us—
  Fresh thy mandate, "Take the light,"
Fix thine image full upon us;
  Send us shining through the night.

Firm we'll grasp the torch pass'd forward;
  Through the darkness bear it skyward;
Know, when flick'ring in our keeping,
  Thy supporting hands of prayer;
Till the nations catch its gleaming,
  And behold the Lord is there!

ROSE GOODWIN POOL (MRS. F. K.)
Class of 1919

197

FIFTIETH ANNIVERSARY HYMN

Dear Alma Mater, great and glorious,
    Once more we come to greet you.
A host rejoicing, glad, victorious,
    Old friends and new to meet you.
Dear Alma Mater, without a peer,
    Our love grows stronger year by year.
God bless and keep you alway.

We love your walls, your spacious halls,
    Your oriel windows golden.
We love the rooms where books are strewn,
    And knowledge is new and olden.
Dear Alma Mater, without a peer,
    Our faith grows stronger year by year.
God bless and keep you alway.

Our faith in you as one whom God
    Has led through all the way,
Has wavered not when you have trod
    A broader, newer highway.
O wonderful the years for you,
    With God's approval shining through.
God bless and keep you alway.

ALICE SHEPARD CARVER (MRS. W. O.)